A Teacher's
Sketch Journal

A Teacher's
Sketch Journal

Observations on
Learning and Teaching

Karen Ernst

HEINEMANN
Portsmouth, NH

HEINEMANN
A division of Reed Elsevier Inc.
361 Hanover Street
Portsmouth, NH 03801–3912

Offices and agents throughout the world

Library of Congress Cataloging-in-Publication Data

Ernst, Karen.
  A teacher's sketch journal : observations on learning and teaching
/ Karen Ernst.
    p. cm.
  Includes bibliographical references.
  ISBN 0-435-08861-0
  1. Creative writing (Elementary education)—United States.
2. Drawing—United States.   3. Notebooks—United States.
4. Learning.   5. Teaching—United States.   I. Title.
LB1576.E76   1997
372.5'2—dc21   97-35415
                                                   CIP

Editor: Toby Gordon
Copy Editor: Alan Huisman
Production Editor: Vicki Kasabian
Book and cover design: Joni Doherty
Manufacturing: Louise Richardson

Printed in the United States of America on acid-free paper
02 01 00 99 98 97 RRD 1 2 3 4 5

For my dad, Devol Elston Ernst,
who taught me the importance of making a contribution.

Contents

Acknowledgments

My sketch journals are filled with drawings and notes about what I have learned from the many people who have contributed to my work as a teacher, a learner, a writer, and an artist. The ideas of Maxine Greene, Nancie Atwell, Don Graves, Regie Routman, and Georgia Heard are the foundation for my thinking and my classroom.

Toby Gordon, my friend and original editor, helps me see and understand my own work in order to be able to share it with others. A wise and informed listener, she helps me get at the heart of what I do. The idea for this book was hers; her urging gave me the courage to make my sketch journal public, to welcome teachers into my classroom.

Alan Huisman, my second editor, was the artist who worked with my words and pushed me to make this book clear, write it in my own voice, make it more than a repetition of former books. His criticism and support while I revised the manuscript rekindled my excitement about the book. Thank you, Alan, for your skill and high standards.

Bill Varner and Vicki Kasabian, my current editors, have seen the book through production with the same high interest and standards evinced by Alan and Toby.

Tom Newkirk has shown a longtime interest in my work. He published my early articles, asked me to speak at conferences, and invited me to develop a course as part of the summer writing institute at the University of New Hampshire. Because of Tom, I was able to approach my work in a more significant way. Thank you, Tom, for inviting me into a community of learners of the highest caliber, letting us turn the foyer of Hamilton Smith Hall into a gallery of art and writing, and providing me a place where I can both teach and learn.

Don Murray, writer, artist, and always teacher, lends strength and conviction to my voice through his interest in what I do. His sketches, his thinking about how drawing the line and writing the line are linked, propel me. His ideas about writing teach me as I sit at my computer. I am humbled to call him both mentor and friend.

Patricia Broderick, at *Teaching Pre K–8*, was quick to recognize that my work was not about art but about literacy. Pat, Alan Raymond, Katie McManus, and Diana Winarski, by inviting me to write a monthly column for the magazine, gave me a wider audience, a way to exercise my public voice, and the discipline to get to the point in less than a thousand words.

The community of Kings Highway School in Westport, Connecticut, gives me a place in which to learn and an opportunity to contribute. Thank you to the principal, Angela Wormser-Reid; the assistant principal, Debbie Fritz-Bradeen; Paul Kelleher, superintendent of schools; and Lynne Shain, his assistant, for their support and for recognizing my need to make my classroom a studio for learning, to teach and learn beyond the boundaries of the classroom, school, and district. They make it possible for me to remain a teacher.

It is in the classrooms of distinguished teachers that we continue to learn. The doors to the classrooms of Dawn Damiani, Elizabeth Olbrych, Kristi Blob, Peter von Euler, Darcy Hicks, Lynn Gehr, Mary Sue Welch, Hallie Cirino, and Dana Larsen are always open. By establishing their own classroom inquiry and talking and writing about their ideas, these colleagues provide the ongoing intellectual stimulation that keeps me excited about teaching. Their work is changing the learning histories of children and teachers. I respect them and am grateful to them.

Thank you, also, to the Community of Teachers Learning, the entire teaching and parent community of Kings Highway, for making it the place where I so much want to be.

When I write I am alone. But there are those who lend an ear or interject a voice when I need it. Thank you to Lad Tobin, for reminding me that if I am not discovering something as I write, writing isn't worth it; to Tom Newkirk, for stressing that when I write, I should not hold back; to Maureen Miletta, for listening to each revision of each chapter, critiquing my voice and encouraging me when I think I just can't do any more; to Kathleen Reilly, for showing me the link between what my students do and what her artist husband, Donald, does in his studio.

In writing, working, and living, I am never really alone, thanks to my life partner, Augusto da Silva. I know what I've written is good when he listens and says, "That's it!" or that it isn't when he asks, "What did you just say?" He was the one, before all others, who said, "This is not about art." He repeated over and over, "Make sure you emphasize the writing and the thinking. Be specific and for goodness sake, get to the point!" His friendship, love, and enthusiasm, and his understanding when I need to be alone to write and when I need to be pulled away to play golf, ski, or vacation, give me the balance I need. He provides the foundation of my work. He is the contributing architect and builder of this book.

With a team like this behind me, I view the publication of this book with humility and a commitment to slow down enough each day to sketch and write whatever is important to me.

1

The Sketch Journal:
A Text for Learning and Teaching

Art gives me time to be real. Art lets me be focused, both as an artist and writer. Art lets the person see what the artist saw and turn into the artist's world.

—Atsuko, age 9

I keep a sketch journal. I take it with me everywhere. Its pages fill up with what I see, hear, think, and feel. I draw and write every day—my cat Pepper as she sleeps, the plants sitting on the windowsill of my classroom, thoughts about school, a plan for a workshop for teachers, a draft of an essay.

I take my sketch journal with me on vacation, where it takes in the tile-roofed houses of Portugal or the woods of New Hampshire. It becomes a record and a memory of what I saw.

I take my sketch journal to a museum to help me read the works of an artist and gather ideas. When I am lucky, pages from the artist's sketch journal are exhibited along with her work. There, I peek inside her thinking, see the drafts of ideas, the sketches that led to the final artwork. I sense the energy she felt, the challenges she faced. I contemplate the process; it feels personal.

But mostly my sketch journal captures the children I teach, my classroom, and the phrases I hear as they create and question.

Each time I start a new one-hundred-page, nine-by-twelve-inch sketch journal, I want to be able to look back and remember this beginning: I picture the moment or draw the place, I copy down a passage from a book I am reading or a statement an artist has made.

My students keep sketch journals too, and as the school year progresses I often begin one of my journals with a quote from one of theirs. Last spring I began a journal with something a fourth grader named Hannah had written in her journal that winter:

Until I was at what you might call the end of my first journal, I never knew what my journal was for. I used to look forward to writing stuff in my journal. I know better now. My journal is a place to put thoughts on paper, sort of like a storage room, until I come fish them out. A journal is also a place to learn about myself. You uncover thoughts you'd never think about. You draw, and drawing leads to writing. Everything is a passage to another link, a never-ending chain. Everything you put down has to be important. It all works together. A journal is a piece of my mind. With this journal, I'm feeling confident that every page will be important. I trust myself.

Keeping a sketch journal links drawing and writing. It helps make my students and me fluent, free of self-consciousness, able to see our own meaning; it teaches us to be better writers, drawers, and observers. Our journals connect us; as we share them, we learn from one another.

My journals model my journey as a teacher, artist, writer, and learner. Together they show how I moved from being a middle school language arts teacher to being an elementary art specialist; they document how I link art to literacy in the artists workshop and beyond. It is important for my students to know that what I am teaching them—to take in the world, to incorporate art and writing into their life and use them to think, discover knowledge, and improve as writers, artists, and learners—is what I am doing.

Drawing My Students In

I take my black pen and begin. I let my pen wander without stopping. I barely look at the page or what I'm putting on it because I am drawing to notice and record, not to make a beautiful picture. Drawing, paying close attention, leads to writing. Writing helps me think, notice more, even discover what I know. Together the pictures and words in my journal help me understand what I know about my students and my practice as a teacher.

The pages that follow the first page are a record of my days. When I look at my drawing of one student, I remember that student, yes, but also the moment, that class period, and the feelings I had. When I reread my journals, I listen to myself rehash a day, fret about the behavior of a class, or worry about the inability of a student to cooperate. I write to figure things out, to discover why things are bothering me, and more important, to discover ideas that will help me solve problems, formulate questions, or take a new course of action. I reread scores of pages written over several months and I see ideas linked to ideas, past situations that inform the present, the seed of theory that has grown into practice in my classroom. Sometimes ideas have developed for over a year in my journal before I implement them in the classroom. My journal helps me take my time.

As we meet on the rug at the beginning of class, I keep my journal open, my pen ready to record what my students answer in response to my many questions about making choices, about linking art to thinking, writing, and learning. I form additional questions that will propel my teaching or note leads for the writing I will ask my students to do at the end of the class. I transcribe conversations.

My students are willing to wait while I get it all down. They know that my journal is a necessary part of my teaching. It is a symbol that I care what they think, that I will do something with their answers, that I am learning with and from them. My practice as a teacher goes into my journal and comes out of my journal. It is where I sketch my plan for tomorrow based on what I notice today. My journal is an aid in creating curriculum; it is my text for learning and teaching.

Keeping a Journal in Company

I am not alone in keeping a journal. Many of the teachers I work with have taught themselves to observe, draw, and improve their writing by keeping a sketch journal. We meet regularly to share the observations we have made in and about our classrooms and to reflect on the meaning and questions that arise in our learning and teaching. We are linked as a group called A Community of Teachers Learning. Our meetings are an opportunity to listen to other teachers, share ideas, admit when things aren't working, and ask questions that propel learning. In so doing, we develop professionally, to the benefit of our students.

Dawn Damiani started keeping a sketch journal and meeting with other teachers at the beginning of her career. She says, "My journal protects me from keeping my wondering inside." Writing about the specifics of a child helps her see the whole child, and that affects how she sees the entire class. Her journal has helped make her teaching and learning purposeful and personal from the beginning. Meeting with colleagues has given her many mentors as well as a forum in which to make her own professional contribution.

Peter von Euler's sketch journal has helped him discover and understand how art and writing are related to scientific observation and to reflective and critical thinking. It is a place in which he and his students can reveal themselves, find their authentic voice. Peter now bases his minilessons on the needs of his students and on the real learning he is experiencing.

There are approximately
100-125 teachers here from all over
state and Idaho, Colorado.
We are now making a picture.
Everyone is (except the two women on the
first row. They chatted and now I hear an
apple crunch. One thing that I can't read is the
energy. Or maybe my reading is that the reading
is no energy. Hard to see faces in here. Hard to be
close to them. I will find out when they share

Tamara
Zollinger

Darcy Hicks draws each student in her third-grade classroom as a way to move in close, pay attention, know that child.

Lynn Gehr rereads her sketch journal in order to help her write the narratives on her report cards. She admits, "If I don't have time to reread my journals, it means I am too busy thinking up new projects for my students."

Journals give teachers a vehicle for ongoing assessment; revisiting their observations lets their own search for meaning and their students' needs drive what they do in the classroom. Through keeping sketch journals and meeting regularly, the teachers who participate in A Community of Teachers Learning continue to experience and understand the role of art in learning, recognize art as significant to our literacy and that of our students, and discover the importance of developing our own meaning as professionals in the essential context of our collaboration. Together we look not only at our students but at our teaching with new eyes; we have come to think of our classrooms as studios of learning and ourselves as artists, learners, and developers of classroom practices.

Changing How We Think of Change

Real change in education is not brought about alone, in single classrooms, by individual teachers. It is brought about when we teachers engage in the literacies we are teaching, when we look back on the work of our students and at our notes and interpretations, when we realize the importance of the role of teacher as developer of classroom practices. When we do that together as colleagues—in all disciplines—we bring about dramatic change.

Then we experience real integration of the curriculum—the overlapping of thought between art, math, science, the multiple lenses necessary to solve problems in learning and life. Then we know how important it is to observe the things that happen in our classroom as a way to make the curriculum grow out of and feed into the needs of the children. Then we define ourselves not as art teacher, reading teacher, math teacher, second-grade teacher, or middle school teacher, but simply as teacher.

The suggestions *observe, slow down, look, think, express, feel confident, find another way, plan ahead, read over, be surprised*, are important in learning and literacy. Making art central to learning and literacy helps us carry out these suggestions. As Donald Graves said in a speech at the 1994 National Council of Teachers of English conference, "Art helps us take in the world, and the best preparation we can do as teachers is read and write." I would add, *and draw*. We have learned that writing should not be the sole responsibility of the English teacher. Likewise, art should not be the sole responsibility of the art teacher. When teachers experience drawing and writing, keep a sketch journal, think of

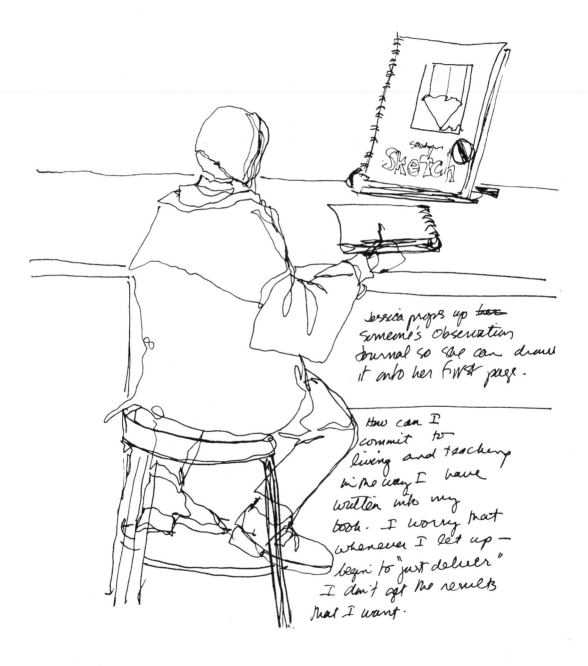

Jessica props up ~~the~~ someone's observation journal so she can draw it into her first page.

How can I commit to living and teaching in the way I have written into my book. I worry that whenever I let up — begin to "just deliver" I don't get the results that I want.

themselves as makers not facilitators of ideas, they find emotion and meaning and discover ideas and thoughts that have been buried.

When our students enter school, they are not afraid to make a picture as a way of telling a story or to raise their hand when we ask, *How many of you are artists?* They know that art is more than being a good drawer. We must look at them with new eyes, listen to them in new ways, and question them about why, how, and when their pictures, thoughts, and stories go together in order for us to understand how the arts can be central to learning—at school and for a lifetime.

When teachers experience what it's like to express themselves by drawing or interpreting a picture and to connect that experience to writing, they understand how their students feel when faced with a task that is frightening or too big a risk. This knowledge changes what happens in their classrooms: teachers make pictures, write, share their pictures and their writing with other teachers, collaborate with the art teacher to integrate art across the curriculum, make their students their informants.

Reading My Journal

This book is about how I make art part of my experience, how I take my passion for art into my classroom and my life, how as the art teacher in an elementary school I have collaborated with classroom teachers to infuse art into the curriculum, what I have learned from my students, how I raise questions, change what I do, and continue to wonder how art can connect with learning in all subjects, in school and in life.

Reading this book, you will visit my classroom—the artists workshop. While you're there, you will observe my students and learn from them. You will listen to their answers when I ask, *How does having choice hurt or help you in the artists workshop? What is art? What do you see? What do you learn from artist's share?* You will find out how a dilemma one day drives what I do the next. You will watch how my personal learning moves from my sketch journal into my classroom. You will learn, as I do, from other teachers who connect art and literacy in their classroom. You'll look over my shoulder into the pages of my sketch journal—get inside my thinking, my questions, the drafts of my ideas, the challenges I face, and my solutions. You'll feel the energy and know that it is personal.

I have not opened my sketch journal for you to imitate but to help you observe your students, wonder, question, learn techniques, paint pictures, try methodologies, translate your experiences and histories, sketch your own plan for a classroom in which art is another form of expression by which you and your students take in the world.

Begin to make your own pictures and write about what you know and re-

Where do you find the passion in your work.

Superintendent's Breakfast

submerged in a task you love ♡

40 new teachers at Westport — In 2 years new staff ½ district wide.

came me at 4 a.m.

Denise Bidey.

Pepper up

Mary Ellen Barry moves to 4th grade.

Taco Bell's Success Story. Making workers independent.

Bom dia.

"It is not enough for a painter like Cézanne, an artist, or a philosopher to create and express an idea, they must also awaken the experiences which make their idea take root in the consciousness of others — A successful work has the strange power to teach its own lesson."
— Maxine Greene

and then asleep by 6:30 a.m.

Release Day Sept. 14

Superintendent's Talk-
Have clear goals
Clarify results
What up based
expect
children to
know.

site-based management.

What is your personal mission for the year. Brings you back to focus & serves as an energy source.

Try orange.

We are information driven. We analyze data based on what we've done. Assess everything we do.

Monday
28

member. Read widely and translate the ideas you find into your own first-grade, fourth-grade, special-education, reading, or art classroom. Share these ideas with other teachers—the teacher next door, in a different grade, in another subject, at another school. Begin the conversation we so badly need in education in order to change what we do and the learning histories of our students.

Imagine me in my classroom with my journal in my hand, the pages open, my black pen either moving across the page, winding around the edge of a student's arm as I draw him, or clipped to the pocket of my white smock, ready to be used. At times I will take a step back to explain why or how I do something, give you ideas about what you can do to learn through experience and how you might translate what I have learned into your classroom and your life.

Begin

Buy a sketch journal full of blank white pages. Write today's date on the first page and begin. Make this first page special, put something there to celebrate the beginning of your journey, the day, and what you are thinking. Record the torrential rains or the political headlines; let your journal reflect your classroom in the context of your life. Suspend any worries about what the page will look like, what it will say. Be aware only that it will help you remember, think, figure things out. Don't be afraid. It is not possible to make a mistake.

Remind yourself that you are keeping a journal not because you want to come up with things to do in your classroom but because you want to think, question, uncover new ideas. Take notes on what you read, quote your students, but make sure you include what you think these things mean. Write down your new ideas—the ones you can take into your classroom and your life—and your questions—the ones that will propel your work, not the ones that will stop you and make you afraid. Your journal is your sketch of what can happen for you and your students. Your plan—your translation of what you see and hear—is what is most important. Your sketch journal is your text for learning and teaching.

Experience for Yourself

- ☐ Look at a tree or a flower or an inanimate object in your living room or classroom. Then discover it by drawing it, giving up all concern about what the picture will look like. Keep your eye on what you're drawing and your pen moving on the page.
- ☐ Write a short piece on what you noticed while you were drawing. How did it feel?
- ☐ Draw something in—or an area of—your classroom. What thoughts or observations or stories does this drawing arouse? Write them down.

- What experiences and passions do you bring to your classroom?
- Recall a lesson, a student, a moment in your classroom. Write about it to bring it back, picture it in words. Consider what this memory means—relook at it. What did you learn? What does it mean?
- For ten minutes observe, listen, and take notes in your own or someone else's classroom. This is an opportunity to learn to see, to practice observing, not a time to judge yourself or your colleague. Relook at the notes, reflect on them. What did you notice? What did you include? leave out? What questions arise? What do you wonder? What does this tell you about you as an observer? Share your ideas with others.
- Make a list of the reasons you want to integrate art into your classroom.
- Write down the reasons you are afraid to bring art into your own literacy.

2

Histories: What Is Basic

I have found through the year that I have improved a lot from the first picture I did of a fall tree and the last picture I did of a kitchen counter. There is a big difference in the two. One has more thought and feeling, but the other feels quick and empty. These pictures show the growth in me as an artist and thinker.

—Ursula, age 10

Open your sketch journal and join me in my classroom—the artists workshop. Watch my students as they work, read over their shoulders as they write, listen as they answer my questions. In the context of your history as a learner, think about the possibilities the artists workshop offers.

Seeing the Possibilities

Gwen stands at the counter of the sun-filled room, working on a collage; around her is the busy activity of a second-grade class. She is a fourth grader and has come to the art room during her recess to continue a series of collages and written messages. The sky she is drawing is a burst of pink and orange; the tiny shape of a bird flies over a black landscape. She has written:

> *Sunrise. Two cactuses and a bird are beginning a new day. The bird is getting food for her young. I see pink, orange, and black. This picture makes me feel warm. I think the message for this picture is: Tomorrow is always fresh.*

All of the students choose their own topics and materials, and because the work is theirs, they often want—need—time to continue. I provide that extra

Gwen always works at Cezanne's counter alone. She has already developed quite a portfolio — her latest picture, which she finished today before painting, is a painted paper collage of a vase of flowers on a table. She added two lines for "a window." Her face turned red as I held it far away and said "Look at this." As she began to paint she looked all around the room — tilting her

time as a privilege, based on a student's ability to come in and work on her own. Choice is accompanied by responsibility, and both deepen the artist's focus and commitment.

Since the artists workshop is a community in which learning occurs across grade levels, beyond time limits, and within a structure that lets everyone know what to do and what to expect, Gwen can work alongside a class of younger students and even conduct a guest minilesson on how writing is essential to her work. This workshop is for both visual and verbal forms of expression. It holds structure, purpose, and possibility.

This class began when the children stopped at the door, read the message on the easel, and moved across the room to the rug. The routine is always the same: meeting on the rug to focus their thinking about ideas and techniques; choosing their topic and material; working on projects individually; sharing as a group and one-on-one; amassing a portfolio; working toward exhibition. The students know they are expected to think about their work and write their thoughts into their artist's notebook or sketch journal. The focus is on learning technique in the context of the ideas, expression, and meaning found in literature and art. It is different from focusing on the product, a beautiful picture. Art for these students is "a new day."

Writing for Meaning

The students in the room focus on their work as recorded classical music plays in the background. Nina, using oil pastels, copies the head of a tiger from a picture book. Brendon sits on the chair near the shelves of books, flipping through pages in search of an idea. Anthony paints a picture inspired by a Henri Rousseau painting, then writes a poem to accompany it. Alexandra sculpts a swan in clay. Robert and Cassie pull clipboards from the shelf and settle onto the rug to copy a picture pinned to the bulletin board. Ideas for pictures come from the books in the room, the art reproductions in the gallery, the other students' pictures on the sharing boards, and the imagination. Surrounding children with literature and art and providing choices—in the workshop or in any classroom—expands the possibilities for expression, establishes mentors, teaches responsibility, and presents challenges for both children and teacher.

Wally takes a box of crayons from the counter labeled *Artist Supplies*, while Courtney settles at her table and places her drawing paper on top of her portfolio. Students know where materials are and have been instructed in how to use them. Structure and routine make this workshop their own. Their portfolios, along with their talk about them, show their progress in the journey they are taking via thinking, learning, and expressing. Courtney finishes her first picture, slips it into her portfolio, and goes over to get another piece of white paper.

steven

The girls
and the
guys in
this class
are very
different.

manna
seems to always
get a book for her
ideas

35

Lindsey is working on collage.
Frank and two other boys are the only male painters.
John and Thomas are drawing guns — and as they
work they make the noise of their drawn guns.

Some children do several pictures in one class; others relish the luxury of working on a picture over time—four or five weeks in some cases.

Wally brings me his picture and asks, "Do you like it?" I take it in my hands and ask him to step back to look at it from a distance. Students learn not to depend on my opinion, to propel their work by being their own critics.

At the end of this one-hour-per-week art class, Andrea hands me a piece of writing she has just finished:

> *Today I made two pictures of two sunflowers. My first one was not very good but I think it had texture. My second sunflower was very good. It had texture and thick yellow strokes. I will make the stem green next art period. I think that picture was good. I was thinking of second grade when we went outside and looked at sunflowers. Van Gogh's pictures inspired me.*

Andrea's writing tells me a lot about her, things I could not determine by merely looking at her pictures. She chose to paint sunflowers based on the minilesson I had done on van Gogh's way of using brush strokes; she can use language to describe her picture and assess her own work; her ideas for pictures come from her experiences, from the talk about artists, and the reproductions hanging in our classroom gallery. Andrea is already planning her work for one week later. Writing as part of the workshop urges my students to think and shows me what they are thinking.

History Lessons

I settle onto a stool at a table with three boys. I am concerned because they appear to be talking more than working on their pictures. My attention moves from the blobs of color and intertwining lines on their papers to their conversation. Jason animatedly describes the picture he is reproducing, a picture he painted over and over in kindergarten. My visual memory brings those pictures back into focus as I capture in my journal the meaning I am unearthing: what I thought were pictures of blobs of color and connecting lines were spaceships running into planets; each planet that was hit burst into a new color. I write questions in my journal about the children's "history" as artists: Do children repeat pictures like professional artists do? Do pictures in their learning history stand out as milestones? The boys watch me as my lines of writing segue into a drawing of the easel by the door.

Like Jason, my history as a learner includes memories of pictures I made all the way through school, pictures that contained stories and meaning. I also remember teachers who recognized that the visual was as important to me as the written word. They helped me have confidence, be a writer, and find my voice.

The artists workshop holds both vision and voice, the students' and mine. It shows how art can and should be central to learning. Connecting art with writing allows me to focus on the thinking and learning of my students and on the meaning in their pictures and projects. It broadens my understanding of my students as learners: I recognize that their pictures and drawings are important expressions of who they are. Pictures are part of their history.

Darker Histories

The histories of many adults—the teachers I meet in workshops—are very different from those of my students. *Good drawer. Not an artist. Projects. Making things. A frill. On the margin. Not basic.* These are the associations so many teachers have with art. Most children enter school wanting and needing to draw, but the time spent in school traditionally changes that desire, buries that need.

When I ask adults to recall an image of a picture they made when they were very young and re-create that picture, some reach for crayons and produce familiar pictures of a house sitting on a strip of green, a partially drawn yellow sun in a corner of the page. For many this was the last picture they ever made, yet they are able to remember the meaning of the picture, where they were when they made it, the details of who they were then, and even what their teacher said about it. Some teachers' eyes fill up with tears when I suggest that they draw. Their stories are jolting.

Pat, an admired and experienced teacher and mentor, was disgraced because of a red bird she made in elementary school: her teacher insisted it had to be blue. Colleen still makes a tree the way her teacher had shown her to make it when she was young: that regimented model has kept her from looking at the way a tree can branch out, grow tall and skinny or short and broad. Teachers tell me that when they were six or seven or nine their teacher told them they would never be an artist. Those words still echo in their ears. Their art was "wrong" and had to be thrown away, which meant throwing away part of themselves.

Other teachers have no experiences to remember. Sharon writes, "Here I am thinking I cannot do anything at all in art, and that art has nothing to do with me. I am totally unpracticed. But if in such a short time I can learn that there is no white space in nature unless it is the sky, that a watercolor wash solves a lot of problems, that I can lie to tell the truth in art as well as in writing, that light changes the color of green leaves in a forest, that a rock is no color that comes in a box, then I am angry." In the process of making pictures in the workshop, she has realized that her history has an enormous gap. She wants to bridge that gap and, through her own experience and learning, bring art to the curriculum of her sixth graders in order to help them see in new ways, to expand their own history.

The vividness of these memories is directly proportional to an adult's fear of picking up a crayon, a pen, a palette, a brush, and facing the blank white page. Sketches in my journal capture Betty beginning a detailed picture of a flower and Ann sprawled on the floor copying the head of a giraffe from a picture book. These teachers began making pictures at thirty-seven, at fifty-eight, in order to relearn what they used to know when they were in kindergarten and have since forgotten. They want to provide new ways for their students to express themselves, to integrate art in their classroom and their life.

Clear Reasons

The art teachers who attend my courses and workshops want to find ways to connect writing to the important thinking and meaning making that goes on in their classrooms. But most of the teachers I encounter are regular classroom teachers, not art teachers. They, too, have clear reasons for wanting to learn about a process approach to teaching art, about integrating art into their curriculum, and about how writing, reading, and art can work together. Here are some of them: to integrate art into science and social studies; because first and second graders begin to write by making pictures; to know how to honor the different sign systems children bring to the classroom; to open the door to reading and writing for children with special needs; to reach struggling readers and writers who can "really draw"; to understand the importance of making decisions and choices; to validate and extend multiple ways of expression.

Philosophers and educators argue for the importance of the arts in school reform: an integrated curriculum releases the imagination. The artists workshop is a blueprint for such a partnership between art and learning, a partnership that includes children, teachers, and parents. It is a metaphor for learning and teaching in any subject and in any grade. It is a picture of what teachers can do and of what childrens' forms of expression can become.

Pictures help my students think, take risks, discover, create, and understand. I reach for the answers my students have given me—the ones I have collected in my sketch journals—to help my adult students learn that art can be—and needs to be—included in learning, that art is part of all of our histories as learners, however young or old.

Changing History

With choice as part of the workshop and art as an ongoing part of their literacy, my students reach easily for a picture from their past and use it to return to a familiar idea, to gauge their own progress. Alexis, age seven, writes, "Today I made a picture of a moon in the middle of the night. I did the picture in first

when I walked into the Annex of 3A
I was welcomed by a burst of
color. Bright tissue paper raised up
from the page of a blotted piece of
paper. Watercolor trays were opened.
Alexis worked on a river and a shore
wall in her sketch journal.
Tommy wrote in his —
while Marc wrote on
a piece of composition
paper.

jars of glue,
markers
and oil
pastel

grade and I wanted to see how I have changed in drawing. My imagination keeps growing. It filled with ideas, then I wanted to draw that picture. I imagined I was standing on someone's lawn looking at a lake and it was nighttime."

When Carson selected a picture from his portfolio that demonstrated his progress as an artist and thinker over the year, meaning propelled his choice. He knew that his picture of a red sun peeking over a thickly painted blue ocean was not his best nor even his favorite: "Maybe boring," he said. But, "If you look at it the other way, it is great. The story behind it is pretty simple. I was on vacation with my family and we went to the beach and saw the sunset. I watched as a flock of birds flew by and passed the sun. That image lasted over a year in my head."

Students know that they need to come to the workshop with an idea, know that they can re-create memories in pictures. Carson and many other students look at their surroundings, remember images for a year, and know that the meaning of a picture, not just the skill with which it is executed, shows their progress.

When writing becomes part of art class, the meaning that students see in their pictures, the choices they make as learners, are clearer to me. Emphasis on process, always in connection with high standards and high expectations, leads to a variety of end products—a picture, a piece of writing, pride. The possibilities of how to see it, capture, it, think about it, say it, are widened. A "basic education" for these students is simple: it includes art, art that is connected to their thinking, their observations, and the other subjects they study.

Finding the Connections

An integrated curriculum is natural when multiple forms of expression are honored. Students prove it when they come to kindergarten and tell their stories with their pictures, and they show us how this integration can continue through the grades when teachers work together, learn from their students, and ask questions about the role of art in learning.

The questions I ask propel my learning about the emerging artists workshop, and I look to my students for the answers. What structures and routines are essential to a workshop approach to learning? Why is choice critical to making a classroom a real workshop, one in which projects are authentic and learning is meaningful? How do art, reading, and writing work together to develop literacy? What do I do as a teacher and a learner, both when I am successful and when I run into problems, questions, and tensions?

When teachers take up crayons or paint and experience for themselves that a picture holds meaning, is not just something someone else will judge, they validate what my students show me every day. When Ann, a middle school teacher, finished her giraffe, she wrote,

Rather than giving us specific drawing lessons, Karen set us confidently on our journey of discovery. I suddenly had no past history. I was able to begin with a fresh slate. I was free to select a subject and a medium. That gnawing habit of comparing and always coming up short was erased. The picture that I was able to copy amazed me, plain and simple. I knew how children felt at the end of drawing something that they really like.

People must first be set on a journey. Only when they are on the journey are they ready for, do they even need, specific drawing or writing lessons. As teachers experience art in their literacy and turn to their own experiences and their own students for answers about how and why this should happen, we will change history, for our students and for ourselves.

Redefining Basic

The artists workshop is filled with the pictures and stories of my students as well as with mine. It is our vision and voice for how art can become a part of all learning, a classroom for the children who need pictures and projects to tell stories, to get ideas for writing, to connect with literature and culture, to see their progress, or to say what they mean.

Look over Gwen's shoulder, watch her create, and consider her message, "Tomorrow is always fresh." Read the thinking of my students and see their pictures with new eyes. Ponder how their pictures of variously shaped trees, of birds flying across the landscape, and of imaginary planets can become part of their learning history.

Children come to school with ideas and need to express those ideas in many ways. When we create classrooms that connect art and writing to all learning and provide structure, high expectations, and choice with responsibility, we create new situations for learning and teaching and redefine what is basic in school.

What is basic to learning, to empowering young people to love learning, and to preparing and changing them for a lifetime is an important question. Are what and how we learned as children appropriate today? I don't think so. The many stories of teachers who fear putting paint to paper show that something is missing. Redefining the basics based on current research, on the work of philosophers and educators, on the knowledge brought by new technology, and on the answers, work, and understanding of our students is a giant step forward. It is complicated, however, because we did not experience these things as part of our basic education. Teachers of the new basics must be learners as well, practicing and doing what we teach.

Art, reading, writing, science, social studies, math, music, physical educa-

Nicholas Anderson painting
a picture from memory of 1st grade – one that
stands out in his history as an artist.

I remember I was really proud of it. And then
I got my idea from Sam DiMatteo and I
remember that it was really good. It was
about a car driving down the road with a
sign and _____ | Today I read from
the book about artists. Their story was our story.
You are in 3rd grade. This artist was discouraged
by something in 4th grade. I know it is hard to
comprehend but you are making history today or
this year. When Nicholas A grows up, will he
write about a picture that he made in 1st grade.

tion, are basic. Overlapping the disciplines is also basic. Schooling must include discrete skills in the given disciplines, yes, but also the skill of looking at a math problem with the eyes of a writer or anticipating the possibilities of science through the eyes of an artist. Children do this naturally until the curriculum and teachers stop them, warning, "Stick to basics, stay within the boundaries."

My vision for the artists workshop comes from a belief in widening the frame of literacy, but my answers are often colored by my teacher voice. My students help me understand the natural connection between art and writing, something many have forgotten since education "wasn't that way when we grew up." I know our students will help us, as we so desperately need to do, redefine what is basic instead of going back to the basics. We need a broader frame of basic, not to exclude but to include: reading, writing, computation, the arts, critical thinking, the imagination. As this frame is widened we will have higher expectations, new challenges, and better results. Education will look different from the way it did when we went to school, the picture will be bigger, will include more children and more ways of saying and doing things.

Experience for Yourself

- What is your history as learner?
- Write about a picture you made as a child. What was the meaning behind it? Why is it important in your memory?
- Draw a picture that you remember drawing when you were a child. Try to make it look just like it did when you were six or seven or nine.
- Describe an image that has lasted with you for more than a year.

3

Organizing the Studio
for Learning and Teaching

Today I watched the sun come up. It is a beautiful sunrise. I said to myself, It is Wednesday. Do I have gym, music, computer, or art? I have art, so I will make a sunrise. I used watercolor and paint.

—Anna, age 7

My classroom is my studio. It is where I teach and where I learn. So that my students can make choices, work independently, learn new techniques, think about their own learning, and anticipate their next art class, I provide a routine, a structure. I want them to arrive with an idea, not wonder what project I will explain.

As you read this chapter, note in your sketch journal your own ideas for *your* room and space, *your* routine and organization, ways *your* classroom can become your studio for learning and teaching—one in which children know what to expect. Specify areas of the room, materials, and routines that will shape your classroom to include the materials of artists and writers, expand the ways children can see and express themselves.

My room is a large fifteen-by-fifty-foot art room. You may be a classroom teacher with a fifteen-by-twenty-five-foot room, a reading specialist with a ten-by-fifteen-foot room, or an art specialist teaching from a cart. The size of my room is not that important. What is important is the areas I designate, how I manage students within the space, and what I want to accomplish. The diagram of the room (see Figure 3–1) will give you the big picture and my notes will explain my reasoning.

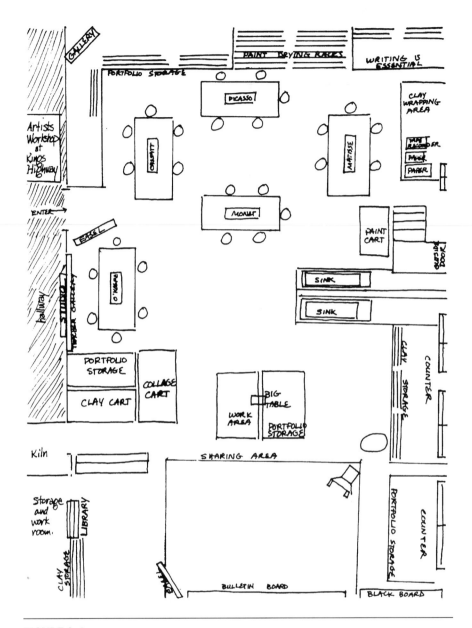

FIGURE 3–1

The Easel

The easel welcomes students to the room, gives them directions on where to go and what to think about as they proceed. Reading the easel is the first literate experience they have as they arrive. The message may be, *What ideas do you have for a picture today?* or *Let's begin with a story to get ideas* or *Be ready for our artist's share.* The message usually ends, *Meet me on the rug.* The underlying message is that there is an important connection in this classroom between literacy and art, between working together as a community, working alone, and knowing where and how to proceed.

Signs and Banners

White signs with bold black letters label things, state principles, or share the words of artists and writers. These signs are part of the landscape of the room, reminding children and visitors what this place is for and inspiring their thinking. *Art Is Basic* or *Welcome to a Place of Excellence* delivers a message. *Artist Supplies, Paper,* tell students where to find things.

The Rug

The rug is where we meet as a class. Everything we do during these meetings is intended to build community. We read a story, look at art, listen to others talk about their work, say what we see, listen to one another to get ideas, learn new techniques. The work in the artists workshop begins here.

The Blackboard

I write the date on the blackboard each day: "Today is [date]." I use the blackboard to remind us of a new day of work and to focus our thinking on the words of artists and writers. Each week I quote from Matisse, Cézanne, Byrd Baylor, Patricia Pollaco, whomever.

I might start a meeting on the rug by reading a quotation aloud: "So I said to myself—I'll paint what I see—what the flower is to me—but I'll paint it big and they will be surprised into taking time to look at it" (Georgia O'Keeffe). Some students copy these passages into their notebook. It shows the importance of the thinking of artists and writers.

A few months into the year I begin quoting the writing of my students. Recently I quoted from Courtney's journal: "To see takes time to look really closely at a picture. At a glance you think what it is but if you take a journey you'll explore things all of the time." This is a form of publishing, it is a way to model how we can learn from one another, and it is a way to create community.

Sharing Board

On the blank bulletin board next to the rug, I pin works from all my classes. This is not a place for the best work only, but a place to show whatever work is

Today is
November
23,
1993

APPRENTICESHIP
LEARNING FROM EACHOTHER

At the rug. The sun blares through the window. Perhaps
this is the beginning of my new phase of writing
and collecting. I need to make this classroom come
alive on paper ———— in words and pictures

Monday/Tues.

22 | 23

going on and to use this work to teach children how to look at, talk about, and respond to art and to give them ideas.

Artist's Share Easel and Chair

When a student volunteers to share her work, she sits in the artist's chair at one corner of the rug while we focus our attention on her picture displayed on the easel in the opposite corner. An artist needs to distance herself from her work in order to see it with new eyes. The artist tells about the work—where she got her idea, how she created it, why she wants to share it—and the others in the class respond with the ideas the work triggers, what they notice and like. This is important to building community and gives students the opportunity to use verbal skills to discuss pictures. And the notes I take on these conversations become an important piece of assessment.

List of Choices

The materials from which my students can choose—crayons, markers, oil pastels, acrylic paint—are listed on a poster next to my chair. Looking at this list as they make their choices helps students decide and gives them an opportunity to read the words. Younger students often walk to the list and point to the choice, an important step in word recognition.

Status of the Class

At the conclusion of each class's initial meeting on the rug, I read the name of each student, who responds by telling me an idea and what material he or she will use to explore that idea. Students may pass when they need a few more minutes; they may also say they are not sure but are ready to go to work.

This commitment to their work confirms the importance of choice and is a one-minute conference—a means of assessment. I can look at the list and notice that a student has been working on a picture for several weeks or is using the same material over and over. The list tells me which students need help dispensing paint or reviewing where ideas come from.

At the top of each status-of-the-class sheet I write the date and at the bottom I write a note to myself about what we did that day in our class meeting—the book we read, the art we looked at, or the new material I introduced. I often also jot down an idea for the next class, a comment about cleanup or behavior (it is much more effective to discuss these issues at the beginning of the next session than at the end of the session in which they occur), or who has asked to do an artist's share. This helps me achieve continuity from one week to the next. Since

I have approximately twenty classes per week, record keeping and note taking are essential to assessment and to keeping the process alive.

Library of Ideas

On the bookshelves near the rug is a collection of several hundred picture books that I have purchased over the years. Students often take a book to their table and copy from it. From time to time a student will sit on the rug and spend the entire class leafing through the books, looking for ideas.

Art Cards

One bookshelf also contains a box of laminated postcards and magazine covers, each labeled with title and artist. Children also get ideas from these prints or take one to the table to copy.

Worktables

Each table is labeled with the name of an artist: O'Keeffe, Matisse, Monet, Picasso, Cassatt. Younger students sit at assigned tables. It helps me learn their names. The older children are allowed to select their work space each time as long as they demonstrate that they are making a responsible choice.

Other Work Spaces

Students often work on the rug when they are copying a picture hanging on the sharing wall or a work displayed on the easel. Some students like to stand along the counter under the window. Students also stand at the glaze cart when they are finishing a clay project.

Gallery

At the opposite end of the room from the rug, near the worktables, is a bulletin board outlined with black paper and labeled *Gallery*. Here I display poster art reproductions, poster-size poems I have copied from books, and quotes by artists and writers. Students come here to immerse themselves in the work of artists and to get ideas for their own work.

Portfolios

Each student has her or his own portfolio, made with two-foot-square oak tag folded in half, which gives a finished size of one foot by two feet. Students keep

Library in the Artists Workshop

all their work in the portfolio. The portfolios are in turn stored in boxes labeled with class codes and kept under counters in the gallery.

Portfolio distribution works like this: Portfolios for students in grades K–2 are also marked with the name of the table at which they sit. This way I can place them on the appropriate tables during the brief time between classes.

Students in grades 3 and 4 find their portfolios on the big worktable and sit at a space of their choice. "Art helpers" in these older grades come down five minutes before class and spread the class portfolios out on the worktable.

Artist's Notebooks

All children in grades 1 through 4 have an artist's notebook/sketch journal, in which they write about what they are doing in the workshop. This notebook is kept in their portfolio unless the classroom teacher and I are collaborating, in which case the students carry it back and forth from their classroom. Writing about their work is an essential part of artists workshop.

Artist Supplies

Artist supplies are kept on two counters. One contains paper in two sizes. Across the room, near the worktables, is another counter with labeled plastic shoe boxes containing labeled plastic cups or boxes of markers, crayons, oil pastels, chalk pastels, colored pencils. A student can take an individual container of these supplies, while the supply lasts.

Writing Supplies

Next to the paper counter are shelves underneath a banner that proclaims, "Writing in the artists workshop is essential." On these shelves are pencils, lined paper, erasers, and black felt-tipped pens. The message and the materials are clear and available.

Storage

Portfolios are stored in boxes, one box per class. Each class has a labeled shelf for clay projects and other 3-D projects. Metal shelves in the work area of the room serve as drying racks; several hundred works can be spread out there on any given day. Boards indicating class code separate one class's work from another's. A small area on one counter is the clay-wrapping area; here students can wrap up their finished clay projects with newspaper and tape and take them home.

Paint Cart

The paint cart stands near the sink. Here students find containers of acrylic paint, watercolors, tempera blocks arranged on a tray, watercolor pencils, and watercolor crayons. Cans of brushes in a variety of sizes are also on this cart. Individual cups for water are at the sink.

Collage Cart

The collage cart contains scissors, glue, and boxes of a variety of papers (tissue paper, construction paper, wallpaper, metallic paper) cut into small squares. Unclaimed paintings or paintings specifically undertaken for this purpose are cut into small squares and used as well.

Clay Cart

Students meet me at the clay cart to receive a piece of new clay (about the size of their fist to begin), a twelve-inch-square masonite board on which they can work at their own table, and a bucket of clay tools (one bucket per table). There is a "return" bucket for used clay.

When I introduce clay, I emphasize experimenting with it, learning to push, turn, and mold it while ideas begin to emerge, not worrying about making something. When a student chooses clay, he must complete the entire process: sculpt something, fire it in the kiln, and paint or glaze it. Painting or glazing encourages students to use their imagination and skill to develop, and in some cases transform, the project—to see it in another way.

Once the clay project has been finished, the student must make a record of it—draw the object and write about what it is, where the idea came from, or what he learned as he worked on it. Drawing the object encourages the student to place it in a context, extend the idea into another art form. Once the record is completed, the student wraps the project and takes it home; the clay record is included in the portfolio.

Music

While students are working independently, I play recorded classical music. Students know they must talk quietly enough so that everyone can still hear the music.

Cleanup

I turn off the music and flick the lights, my signals for quiet and attention. "Be ready to leave in two minutes." Plastic cups of materials are returned to the bins on the artist supplies counter, used clay is placed in the "return" bucket, wet paintings are laid on the drying rack. I stand at the sink and wash palettes and brushes as students drop them in. When the students have put away all their materials, they return to their worktables and raise their hands.

When students are invested in what they are doing—when they are working on something they have chosen to do—they cleanup quickly and efficiently: they want more time in which to work. When cleanup procedures need to be reviewed, I do it in a minilesson.

Teaching children where things are, how to use materials, and how to clean up is important if your workshop is to be an ordered place for independent and responsible work. A routine establishes limits but also encourages students to make the workshop their own. When children—or adults, for that matter—know where things are, know where to get ideas, and know how to get started, they develop a sense of ownership that prompts more responsibility and greater confidence. In a workshop structured in this way—one in which there is a feeling of comfort and safety—continued minilessons, shared ideas, and raised expectations help the students take risks, experiment, learn from their own mistakes, and begin to value what goes on there.

Experience for Yourself

- Draw a diagram of your own room. How is each area used? How might areas be used differently?
- List the materials available for student work.
- Sketch a new plan for your classroom.

4

Building a Community

During my time in the art room I have learned many things, like to look more closely at the veins of a leaf. I also learned that however hard you try you'll probably never get something right on the first try. You have to look harder and cross things out and do them over until you're satisfied.

—Samantha, age 9

When visitors come to the artists workshop, they invariably copy a hand-lettered sign that hangs midway in the classroom. It reads:

In the artists workshop we:

- Bring our own ideas for work.
- Make choices about what we use.
- Talk with quiet voices about our work.
- Think about our work as we make it.
- Share our work to help teach others.
- Respond to the work of others.
- Try new things and try our best.
- Write about what we think, feel, observe, learn, and discover.
- Clean our space to leave it in order for others.
- Observe the world around us because observation is at the heart of our work.

After watching classes meet me on the rug, make choices, and go to work, the visitors ask, "How did you get the children to talk about another student's work with such respect?" "There is such focus as they work. What did you do or say?" "How do you get the children to clean up in two minutes?" "What are the important minilessons?" "Where do you begin?"

No poster on the wall, no book, can explain or prescribe what I do. The essence of my approach lies in the expectations I establish, ones that are higher now because of the history of the students who have come before. It stems from an early focus on building a community in the classroom—one in which students, teacher, and parents are all learning and teaching. It resides in how I prepare for my days of teaching—reading, writing, and drawing—in how I reveal my own learning, and in my constant need to question my students and myself, assess often and in varied ways, and take action on what I learn.

Bring your sketch journal to the rug. Sit in a chair opposite me as one class after another begins building our community, a community that focuses on getting ideas, looking, listening, telling our stories, realizing that we must experiment and take risks in order to develop expertise. Take notes on the first sessions of the school year to see where we begin, how we head in the right direction.

The Importance of Talk

My focus during the first session is on thinking together, listening to one another, and talking about ideas. I greet a class of first graders as they settle onto the big red rug, eager to return to their work in the artists workshop. Their eyes stare at me.

"How many people in this class still have imagination?"

They all raise their hand and a few giggle as mine goes up as well.

"Whew," I say with relief, "this will make our job much easier." I establish that we must learn to think, talk, and listen in order for the classroom to be a community in which we learn from one another.

I hold up the book *I Am an Artist,* by Pat Lowery Collins, illustrated by Robin Brickman. The illustrations show billowing clouds and bursts of sunlight hovering over a green, hilly landscape. I choose this picture book because I want my students to know that being an artist is looking at the world, creating and designing with the mind, thinking about what things can become, and using the imagination. I want them to understand that art is a part of living, it is experience, and it is connected to learning in many ways. I want them to know that artists need to read literature and that together pictures and words tell a story.

This kind of beginning to the "art class" is very different from a lesson on how to do something. I am aware that what I do, what I read, what I show, are as important in my teaching as what I explain, what I direct, what I assign, what I say. All of these things, taken together, create expectations, deliver a message to slow down, ask us to think about what we will do.

I continue. "Let's review the artists workshop. Can someone tell us what it is?"

In the Artists Workshop we:

- [ ] Bring our own ideas for work.
- [ ] Make choices about what we use
- [ ] Talk with quiet voices about our work.
- [ ] Think about our work as we make it
- [ ] Share our work to help teach others.
- [ ] Respond to the work of others.
- [ ] Try new things and try ours best.
- [ ] Write about what we think, feel, observe, learn, & discover
- [ ] Clean our space to leave it in order for others
- [ ] Observe the world around us because observation is at the heart of our work.

mini lessons be. signs become parts of room

Clean-Up Sign as a Reminder

Mini lessons in the beginning
- Get ideas
- Routine
- Talking
- Clean-Up
- where to put wet pictures
- where materials are.
- Clean-up.

Techniques
- watercolor.

Thinkers
Books — artists Share

Matthew's answer, "It is about concentration," surprises and pleases me. His former experience here has taught him that the work is about paying attention, not so much about making things.

The first session ends the way it began—with thinking and talking. I click off the music and flick the lights—my signal that I have something to say. After a quick cleanup, I suggest, "Let's pretend we are going to write about our work here today. Would anyone like to tell us what he or she learned, or did, or discovered today?"

"I made a castle." "I made a dinosaur." "I found out how to make a new color." "I made a picture of when I went to visit my grandpa's farm." "I made a pretty picture." "I had fun."

In the first session I use many opportunities to talk and to get students to be aware of their own thinking, creating, and personal learning. This prepares them for later minilessons on keeping an artist's notebook/sketch journal and making writing part of the workshop routine.

Beginning with an Idea

I teach and review where ideas come from. "Let's review where we get ideas other than from our experiences—the ones we bring to the workshop in our imagination." Pointing out all the things that can help students get ideas—the books, the classroom gallery of art reproductions, physical objects, nature—is as important as showing how to use watercolors, oil pastels, and clay. I show them the spaces in their workshop.

They listen intently as I review the "library of ideas." I encourage them to take a book off the shelf and read it for ideas or take it to their work space and copy one of the pictures. When a student wants to know what a tree or dinosaur looks like, we reach into the shelves to research how another artist has depicted it.

The box of art cards is another place we can search for ideas. Just as art students go to a museum to copy the work of the masters, we can learn ideas and techniques by copying the work of artists. I walk to the other end of the workshop, to our classroom gallery, where a variety of art posters are displayed.

I continue my tour of the room, guiding students to possible ideas. I point to green plants on the window, Raggedy Ann and other stuffed toys on cabinets, or a jar of brushes. I encourage them to draw what they see. I point out the sun-filled window and suggest that they look around for ideas outside the classroom—on the bus ride home, when they play in the yard.

"What have I forgotten?"

Eager hands go up. "Things from our imagination." "Ideas from my head."

It is important to talk about using our imagination, because it is something we rely on in art, reading, writing, critical thinking, math, science, in all learning.

Learning Routine: Committing to Work

Teaching routine is important so that students know the limits and expectations within which they can create. (I also teach the expected routine to the classroom teachers, so that they feel welcome to participate and can help their students make important connections between their classroom and art.)

I begin teaching the expected routine as soon as students line up at the door of the art room with their classroom teacher. I expect them to wait while their teacher helps small groups of children read the message on the easel. The message on the easel—"What ideas do you have for your work today?"—shows the students that coming with an idea is part of the routine.

Commitment is a vital part of the routine. After reading a book, talking about some aspect of art, or doing a minilesson on how to use a material, I reach for the clipboard on which I keep my class lists and record what each student will do that day.

Making a thoughtful choice is part of my expectation. In the beginning the choices of materials are limited to markers, crayons, pencils, oil pastels, and pens. Working with familiar media keeps the focus on expressing ideas. Reading the name of each student in the class, asking her or him to say out loud what topic and material she or he will use, provides others with ideas, requires all the students to make a verbal commitment to their work, and gives me a record of what each student does over time.

Courtney chooses markers, Brendon says, "I'll look at a book," Deborah requests crayons, and Wally tells me, "I'll make a picture of a camping trip I am going to take." Andrew looks at me with indifference and says, "I don't know what to make today."

After the other children get started at their work space, I do a follow-up minilesson with Andrew on how to get an idea. I do not tell him what to make. We walk hand in hand to the library of ideas, the art cards, the gallery, and spend time looking around the room. My whole-group teaching and my teaching of individuals confirms what I believe: that choice is central to the workshop and that finding an idea is a necessary skill.

Repeating minilessons on the classroom routines with an individual student—how I expect her to use her time, the kind of talk about work and process that is appropriate in the workshop, the signals I use when I want him to listen, how to place a wet picture on the paint drying rack quietly, what to do when finished with a picture or project, how to clean up responsibly and quickly, the mechanics of dismissal—helps make the workshop a place of focused work. Teaching routine establishes expectations, provides an atmosphere in which choices can be made, and encourages experimenting and risk taking.

The Stories We Tell Teach

I show my students my own work as an artist and writer. The stories I tell about my own risks, mistakes, and successes teach them lessons that they take to their own work.

I open a journal that I kept during the summer while on vacation in Portugal. "I always take a journal with me." By opening the pages of my journal, I establish myself as a writer and artist. I reveal who I am to my students. I pay close attention to breakthroughs and silences in my own work as an artist and writer so that I can better understand the breakthroughs and silences of my students. Constantly drawing, writing, reflecting, I uncover ideas for mini-lessons.

"This summer I set out to make a very beautiful drawing. I was in a tiny village where the blue sky was in contrast to the dark green pines, the orange tile roofs, and the white stucco houses. There were flowers everywhere; there were chickens and goats and no one was around. I was nervous. Because I wanted my picture to be so beautiful, I kept searching for the right subject. I couldn't find anything to draw!" The silence of my audience, their focused looks, told me they understood, that it had happened to them.

"Then I said to myself, *Wait a minute! You tell your students there is always something to draw. You just aren't looking hard enough.* I sat on a rock and decided just to look and draw. I forgot about making a beautiful picture; that would come in time. In order to make a beautiful picture, you have to just sit still. You have to do that a lot."

The stories we tell our students and the stories we tell other teachers about our classrooms teach and inform in many ways. Most important, they show our students that we are not asking them just to do something—make a picture, sculpt in clay, write a story—but that we are asking them to strive to let their work matter, because what we do matters to us.

I show my students that I need two forms of expression—drawing and writing—that my journal helps me notice things, and that noticing things is part of my life. Home, school, the artists workshop, are not separate things for me, and I want to establish that what I teach them, what they experience here, has changed my life and I intend for it to change theirs.

I also want my students to know that I am learning from them, that I will draw them into my journal, ask them questions, and I hope find answers about the connections between art and writing and all learning. This is the foundation for a learning community, one in which we can all be teachers and learners. I show my students that at times I need to sit on the rock and look. I teach them to see.

Learning to See

I must teach my students to slow down, look, and think about what they see. I place several pictures created during the first few weeks of artists workshop on the blank board.

"Let your eyes focus on the pictures for a few minutes." A hand goes up, but I ignore it. "Let's do this in silence. It is important to think about what you see, why your eyes stop at a certain picture. Think about what you notice, what you learn. I'll time you. After two minutes I'll say okay. Then you may raise your hand and say what you notice."

After two minutes, hands go up. Stephen says, "This one kind of makes me feel bright and happy."

"I like this one because it makes me feel like . . . a flower!" Lila responds.

Emma hesitates as she speaks, and we wait for her thinking to emerge. "All of these pictures . . . are unique. Not one is alike."

"This one makes me think of swimming on the beach," says Nick.

If I am going to expect children to think about their own pictures, get ideas from other children, and respond to the work of professional artists, I must teach them to be quiet, look, say what they see, and be aware that they are entitled to new ways of seeing, interpreting, and expressing. Building a workshop community means that I must teach them how to respond to one another and how to listen to another person's ideas. This prepares students for "artist's share," in which a student volunteers to share his work in progress and get responses, a process that further builds community in the art room.

If I want them to understand that copying is a way of learning—and that this is what happens when writers and artists meet and discuss their work—I must teach them that imitation is not taking away from but adding to another person's ideas. Learning to look at and talk about the work of others must come before working and writing ourselves.

Designating Experts

I teach technique and hold up children's work as exemplars. I use student work in minilessons to show expertise, to show what is possible.

Val's picture of a winding road in front of a row of houses and barns against a lavender sky is displayed on the bulletin board by the rug. I show the picture book from which he got his idea. I explain how Val made the picture over and over in different sizes, how he used a combination of crayon and watercolor, a technique called "crayon resist."

Val's friend Carl worked by his side; when Carl shares his drawing, he acknowledges that his work has changed because of Val's. Students in other classes copy Val's picture, doing their own versions in watercolor, in black pen, smaller, bigger, making it their own. For these students, Val is an expert—an artist like the ones whose work is displayed in the gallery, a source of inspiration.

A lion, the head of a giraffe looking upward, a landscape defined by a fence, a deer in the forest, a tiger—these pictures are celebrated for their student creator's expertise and become a model for others.

Designating classroom experts extends the idea of apprenticeship to include students and teachers in all grades. Students sprawl on the rug, copying the work of other students. A student takes her picture and writing into another classroom and conducts a minilesson on how she made the picture, got her idea, wrote about the picture. Designating a lot of experts propels student work; establishing only a few students as "good artists" or "good writers" slows it down. When a student's work is shared or he does a guest share, his work is propelled as well. This is both essential to and a result of building a community of shared learning.

Learning from Experiments and Mistakes

I teach my students that artists need to experiment and work with their mistakes. I read to the class from Justin's notebook:

> *I say I'm going to make an antelope head out of clay. I tried to make the head, but it was too hard. I tried to make a wolf. Way too hard for me. I tried to make a tree, but it caved in. It looked like a tree stump, so I said to myself, Tree stump with a bird hole.*

I read this to encourage experimentation when trying a new material, to create an environment in which students are not so quick to give up or throw something away because it is not "right." When I introduce clay, I suggest that my students take an entire hour to push and turn the clay, to create shapes, then roll the clay back into a ball. I encourage them to experiment with creating colors when they work with paint.

I want my students to take risks, try new materials, not limit themselves to the same choices. Trying something new can be frightening.

Liz, a second grader, chooses paint, her least favorite material, for the very

Student Gallery

Learning from
the experts.

What ideas do you get as you look at 3rd & 4th grades work.

26 I like the giraffe and the monkeys. I would add them together.

I'm going to do trees & monkeys and giraffes in same picture.

I like the giraffe and I think it really looks like one.

I like the one with the colored sky and the trees.

I like the detail —

Chalk pastel pictures can turn out really great —

I looked at the giraffe — back & front — diff angles

first time, then writes, "Today I think, I think I got an eensy, weensy, teensy little bit better at painting." When a student learns to try her least favorite thing and then is able to see a little progress, she has made a giant stride in learning—not about paint or painting or even writing, but knowing that she can take a risk.

Unloading Pictures, Loading Up Questions

In a workshop in which children make choices, use a variety of materials, and express themselves in many ways, I must have clear expectations for my curriculum. My minilessons teach those expectations—thinking, listening, talking, coming with an idea, learning from others, making mistakes, experimenting, and honoring good work.

My students, both through what they make and what they mean, inform my classes as they form the art room community. I therefore need many forms of assessment, not merely those that evaluate the status quo but those that will help make the workshop alive and changing. A minilesson for a day or a class suggests itself as I observe my students, worry about what I do not understand or like, draw and write for myself, and identify the skills and lessons I need to teach. My plan comes from my vision of the artists workshop as a community of learning. My curriculum includes art history, techniques in using a variety of materials, and reflections on the learning process.

Early in the morning, before the students arrive, I prepare for a day in the life of a workshop. I take the stools off the tables, change the date on the blackboard, pull out the portfolios for the first class, and write a new message on the easel. I read back over the pages of my sketch journal and the notes written on my clipboard class list to remind me of what I have learned, where the class left off the last time we met.

As I open the paint drying racks to reveal the pictures from the day before, I assess my students' learning. The splashes of color in several "splatter paintings" make me wonder about intention—experimentation or play? Was this painting half-finished because it had been only partially thought out, or was its creator just not thinking at all? The questions I ask, the tension, my feeling of being off balance, propels what happens next.

I find two paintings in which tiny details are confined to the bottom of the page. There is a huge empty distance between the ground and a thin blue line across the top of the page. I do not like what I see, but what I see is only part of the picture.

I make assessments as I examine the shelves where the clay projects are stored, as I glance through student portfolios, as I review my status-of-the-class lists. Has James chosen the same material over and over? Why hasn't Ellen ever painted?

I assess my students as I move around the classroom, asking them questions, taking notes, drawing them at work, and reflecting on a day that has been exciting or challenging or disappointing. What I write in my journal leads me to question and to change:

- How can I teach new skills, improved techniques?
- What happens when a student chooses the same medium or topic over and over?
- How can I help my students recognize and understand the influence that professional artists and writers, their fellow students, and I have on them?
- How can art be a means of expressing new learning and thinking?
- How does student writing reflect thinking and learning?
- How can what we do in the artists workshop impact the learning of the child across the curriculum and for a lifetime?
- How can I assess my students more effectively?
- What happens when children are offered choices?

The questions I raise for myself help me question my students. Their answers are a form of assessment. I try to ask questions to which I do not have answers: therefore, my students know they have a real stake in our collective learning.

I assess my students when I ask them to review their portfolios at home with their parents. I assess what parents tell me when they visit the artists workshop. A mother of a kindergartner told me that her daughter now proudly talks about how she "inspires" her friend's work instead of being angry because her friend is copying.

I assess students when I discuss a child with his classroom teacher in the hallway. I assess a student as she shares her picture and process with the class. I assess the class and individuals in it as they respond to their classmates and their classmates' pictures.

I assess my students by what they select for an all-school exhibition and by what they sketch when we go into the hallways to view the exhibition.

Student writing is also a form of assessment. It reveals intentions, frustrations, successes, and experiments.

Assessment is a review of the work my students have done and a preview of the work they will do. New questions begin each new year. Assessment begins the first day of class. On that first day, I begin to create a community in the classroom. My questions and tensions, the observations in my sketch journal, drive what I do and help me establish expectations. I want my workshop to be a place where both students and teacher will grow, learn, and change.

Experience for Yourself

- How do you model your own work as a learner?
- What are the indications or visible signs that show who you are, what you believe in and expect?
- What are the ways in which you build your classroom community?
- What are the expectations you have for your classroom community?
- What routine, what structure, enables your students to create and learn?

5

Art and Writing: A Partnership

My talent as a writer lets me go into deep dark places when it is light out. It lets me explore nature when I'm just sitting on my bed. I can go across the sea with just a touch of my pen on paper.

—Ann, age 9

I flick the lights and turn off the music: "Clean up and be ready to write." Students sit at the five tables in the work area. Writing and sharing will take us to the end of this session of the artists workshop.

Writing establishes that reflecting on the picture and the process is an important part of what goes on here. It allows the students to follow up on ideas that we discuss at the beginning of class or ones that I suggest to them as they work. Writing about and sharing ideas confirms community—everyone has something to say. It supports the belief that thinking is at the heart of the artists workshop.

Open your sketch journal and get ready to jot down your thoughts as I guide this class through a writing session.

Expectations

"Where did you get your idea for your work today? What did you discover as you worked? Try to use words to show the picture you made. If there is some other idea you want to write about based on your work in the art room today, you may do that too."

I make my expectations about writing clear: *This is time for us to think and put that thinking into words. See if you can keep your thoughts coming and your pencil moving. Try not to stop writing for the entire five minutes. Do not worry about spelling or even if your writing makes complete sense. You may find that you need to move from one topic to another. Right now we are learning to think on paper,*

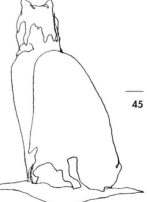

develop and exercise our skill as a writer. Do not talk and please do not move around the room.

Writing at the end of art aims toward fluency and spontaneity in describing the meaning in pictures and process. While most students slip their picture into their portfolio or onto the drying rack, some keep their picture on the table in front of them. They need to see it to write about it. Steven glances at his chalk pastel picture of a scribbly red barn against a background of green. David holds his picture of the bright orange face of a fox in one hand while he writes in his artist's notebook with the other. Someone sharpens a pencil; someone else leaves for the rest room. The room is silent.

I model my expectations as I sit with the class and write. As the year progresses I return to my expectations. I want students to move from discomfort to comfort in expressing their ideas in writing.

When I introduce the artist's notebook as part of their work in the artists workshop, I ask that students use it to think about their work, record what they do, write ideas for next time, or write about their picture. I explain that drawing and writing in the artist's notebook are both acceptable; I use my own sketch journal as a model.

It is especially important for first graders to know they can draw a description if they are not yet ready to write. Most use their artist's notebook to practice their new craft of words, sounding out letters and inventing spellings that describe their pictures. As younger students read their words back to me, I write them in standard English on a Post-it. First graders share with their teacher first before sharing with the whole class.

My expectation for older students is that they use the artist's notebook primarily for writing, in poetry and prose. They need time to exercise their skills as writers. Writing, along with pictures and projects, becomes an art form, a choice in the artists workshop as the year progresses. There is constant tension for me in how to help the student who only wants to draw to write, and the one who only wants to write to make a picture. Pictures and writing inform each other.

Showing Thinking

After five minutes, I interrupt the silence. "Would anyone like to share? Try to select a line of your writing that will let us know what you were thinking today. Make sure you read with a clear and loud voice so everyone can hear you."

Sharing ideas, hearing the voices of children, builds a classroom community. Sharing can occur in a variety of ways: have each person quickly tell what he or she wrote about; call on volunteers; survey topics by asking for a show of hands; ask the class to reread what they have written, underline a sentence or

describe what you
you drew. Use
language so that
we can see
it through
your words.

what were you thinking
as you drew? What
did you notice about
you or the object?

☐ Capture the moment of what
     we just did.
☐ what memory came to
     you as you drew?

your choice.

phrase that creates an image—one they think we can see—and then read that sentence or phrase aloud; ask one student to share a sentence and have other students read a sentence from their own writing that they feel is related. Sharing writing aloud is a good exercise in really listening, in rereading, in rethinking.

Today, Steven reads first: "In art I made a picture of my grandfather's barns. It was kind of hard to make, but I did it." In a minilesson I had talked about how a picture can recall a memory.

David announces his pride in making his fox. "This fox is my breakthrough. It was the first time I tried to copy a picture from a book, and I was successful." David's language mimics what I have said in a meeting on the rug. Writing about their work allows students to go public with their progress.

Student writing shows me when they are struggling: Chris is upset because I did not notice his picture, Samantha's work in clay is frustrating. Writing as part of the work in the art room helps me celebrate progress and offer assistance when it is needed. It provides me with a bigger picture of the child and his work.

Writing encourages students to plan ahead and reveals that ideas have many sources. Nicholas's idea came from a unit of study in the classroom, and he is planning for next week: "A few weeks ago we dissected barn owl pellets. Today I started a picture of a great horned owl. I still need to make the tree and finish the body." Cary clips a small "reminder" to her portfolio; the intertwining squiggly lines of color are her idea for her next picture.

Writing reinforces the responsibility to come to art with an idea. Jane writes, "Even on Saturday I knew what I was determined to do in art on Monday. I knew clearly that I was going to draw a flower with marvelous pink petals with no straight edges and a stem filled with all shades of green."

Gwen's notebook reveals the complexity of the artistic process, that ideas for pictures develop in the process of making pictures and writing about them. She uses the time at the end of art to sketch and write a plan for her next picture, of her skiing vacation in Utah, noting the colors she wants to use. Then she searches *National Geographic* for ideas for a collage. Finally, she writes about the picture she calls "The Haunted Moon": "When I put some black against the blue, it made it look darker and more mysterious. Finally I added the tree, which gave the moon a feeling that it was covered up, and I thought that it was haunted."

Writing helps students spend time with their picture and gives credence to their individual process. It also reflects the learning students gather from mini-lessons—experimenting is important, making mistakes is okay. Samantha writes, "I learned that you don't have to do something the very first time you do it. For example, today I tried clay for the very first time this year. Everyone else did something, but I was experimenting so I didn't make anything."

A day of breakthroughs in '2G.
Sebastian's bird, Ryan's lion.
Mrs Cehr's beach memory,
Nicole's writing comes alive!
Nicole thought of her writing
and that's why she made me
lion. She didn't know what to
write if she ~~went~~ did the fox.

A workshop in which students come with their own ideas, are in charge of their time, and must think and write about the process is truly theirs.

Leads and Prompts

Leads for writing most often come from our discussions at the beginning of each class—our reactions to a passage in a book, our response to an artist's share, our reasons for selecting a picture for an exhibition. Here are some leads I use:

What do you see in your picture?

What do you feel as you look at your picture?

What is the story in or beyond your picture?

If you went inside your picture, what would you find?

What inspired you?

What are your plans for the next workshop?

What surprised you or what did you discover as you worked?

What is happening in your picture?

Leads for writing also grow out of my questions as I watch students work or listen to their conversation. How do fourth graders use drawing as part of their writing process? Where and how do they gather ideas? Why are they sometimes unfocused?

I ask a class of fourth graders, "Why do you draw?" Steven answers, "I draw because my teacher wants me to write and I don't get any ideas to write about if I do nothing. . . . It also gets me to try other things, not only art things, but things to do in life. It helps me to figure out a fraction problem. It helps me with my life."

When I ask about the partnership of art and writing, Rogan writes, "How do I make room for myself? By making art. I can make my thoughts real. Only in art can I express myself. Only in writing can I explain."

Responses like these help me focus on what I say at the beginning of a workshop, what the students are working on, and the process of developing a classroom community. Writing helps me ask questions, find answers. It helps the workshop change and grow.

Picture This

A picture is an experience, a bridge to thought. First grader Jillian writes, "I am on the beach. The palm trees are next to me. The water is calm. A sailboat is sailing. The sun is shining. There is a sunset." Fourth grader Nicholas draws tornados over and over. In one picture, a tiny red house sits on the line of green field across the bottom of the page. The gray swirling sky fills the rest of the page, a charcoal funnel twisting to the top. He writes,

> When I grow up I want to be a meteorologist because I want to experience the weather. The more I draw pictures of what I want to be when I grow up the more I feel like that already. When I drew, I felt like I was watching out the bedroom window watching how the tornado would spin and pick up things from the air and bring them high up in the sky.

A picture is a means of recall. The process of making the picture brings the moment and the details into focus. Marc's picture of two trees against a blue sky is a memory of going to the park to have picnics with his mom:

> I got my idea for my picture from a memory of when I used to go to the park and have picnics there. I remember when my mom would push me on the tire swings, she would push against the logs on the side (I called it a bumpy ride). I'd go on the swings, close my eyes, pump, and when I felt like I was high I'd open my eyes.

A picture is an image. Writers and artists see and use images. Writing connected to art helps students understand this. They collect images as they look for ideas, record these images in pictures, then capture the images in writing. We see Rogan's image in her words:

> When I was on my way to school today, I saw a black duck sitting on a peak. He seemed to be black as midnight. Behind him was a carnation pink sky with gray clouds here and there. He was sitting above a river with his head up. He seemed to be a king looking out on a river which connects to the silent, calm Long Island Sound.

Pictures are a springboard and a partner, they lead to writing in natural ways. Spending time with the picture—creating it, thinking about it, writing about it—leads to the details and memories within. Writing pushes students to collect ideas and form images. It is a bridge to the classroom experience.

Making the Connections

Classroom teachers come to the artists workshop, just as you have, and write with their class or listen as their students share. They believe the voices their students reveal in the context of their art are different from the voices they use in the regular classroom. Many of these teachers ask their students to take their notebooks or sketch journals back to the classroom; there they write for sustained silent periods about their pictures and their processes in art.

Writing goes beyond the last five minutes of art, and art goes beyond the confines of one hour per week. The thinking that occurs in the studio, the ideas held in a picture, the images that children collect, find their way into writers workshop and across the curriculum. The learning that occurs in art is stretched as fourth graders write for twenty or thirty minutes or more about their picture. First- and second-grade teachers teach writing using the ideas in their students' pictures. The art studio and the classroom, too long separated, are linked.

When Rogan takes her sketch journal back to Paula Mirto's fourth-grade classroom, she opens it to the picture she made in art. It is a black silhouette of a tree against a divided background, blue sky and pale moon on one side, pinkish sky and an orange rising sun on the other. She writes:

Between the dusk
When the sun has begun to appear
When the twilight is old
And the day is new
Where the morning is very near
When the mountains guard
The sweet horizon
When the morning doves will sing
Just as the twilight
Flies away
The morning's about to take wing
When the forest
Of fortune and fate
Is touched by the sun so bright
Most of the flowers
So withered and dark
Are suddenly filled with light
The mountains so cold
The trees so dark
Have suddenly all turned bright
That is my picture
That's how it goes
When it turns from darkness to light.

What possibilities open in a collaboration between the classroom and the art room.

Art in the Writers Workshop

Many writers workshops now begin with pictures. Teachers have not added an artists workshop to their already busy schedule and curriculum but have revised and restructured their writers workshop to include and value art as part of the writing process. They no longer ask children to let go of making pictures in order to learn to write or suggest that pictures should only "illustrate a story."

Just as writing in the artists workshop propels thinking and expression, making pictures in the writers workshop leads to better, more natural writing with a wider range. Students begin telling their stories by making pictures. Using art supplies and making pictures are valued choices in writers workshop. Art expands the writers workshop.

Mary Sue Welch finds that her first-grade writers workshop has a new focus—students waste little time, have a wider source of ideas for their writing, writing forms have expanded beyond the forced "story" she used to require. With pictures a valued part of the process, those students who struggle with writing have more ways to achieve success and make a bridge to writing.

First grader Victor is a full participant in the writers workshop through his pictures; he tells his stories and gets responses from his classmates. This increases his confidence and leads him to write ideas about the pictures. He is able to avoid the "good drawer but not so good student" label that so many children obtain as early as first grade and never lose.

Making a picture teaches observation—a quality necessary to good writing. During Lynn Gehr's second-grade writers workshop, Margaux makes a picture of the rain on the field outside the window of her classroom. Her focus leads to a poem about the storm:

RAIN ON THE FIELD

A dark cloud forms
in the sky in a flash.
The rain splashes down in
the ground where all
is calm and peaceful.
The sky turns blue to black.
The sun folds into
the sky. The rain
is coming.

Pictures lead to poems and metaphorical writing. They expand the possibilities of writing to include description, poetry, reflection, and analysis as well as story.

Pictures are a record. Linda Stern shows a picture from her own journal to her kindergarten class and many months later finds a replica of that page done by one of her students. She learns what her kindergartners already know, that a picture is a story, that a picture holds a memory. Her experience with making pictures and keeping a journal leads her to recognize and encourage the natural balance between pictures and beginning writing. The results are more kinds of writing and more enthusiasm for learning to write.

Pictures Continue in Process

Some students in Peter von Euler's fourth grade need to paint for a few minutes at the beginning of the writers workshop in order to focus themselves and get ideas. Their pictures are not directly connected to the writing they then do but get them ready for the process. When Sarah spends time writing about her watercolor swirls, it helps her "learn about my picture. I didn't think it looked like a dance until I began writing a poem about it. Then I thought of it differently."

Chelsea explains, "It helps me to draw a picture before I write. It helps when I get stuck somewhere in the middle of a story. I draw a picture of what has already happened or will happen. It helps me imagine what things look like." Pictures push Sarah's writing when she is bored: "I always look outside at the trees or something with branches and I imagine something in the branches like a face or an object or a part of a story happening."

Art helps students like Justin, who struggle with writing, find their voice, achieve success: "Last year I doubted myself on most pictures but my last picture was my favorite. Two birds. Just two birds on a big piece of paper."

The art-writing partnership helps third and fourth graders express themselves in a variety of ways. Creating pictures plays a role in their writing process, opens their imagination, and helps them find their writing voice.

Extending the Connections

The connections between art and writing lead to other connections. Teachers restructure their writers workshop, students keep sketch journals, students share their art and writing in other classes and with other grades. Classes form a buddy relationship with a class at another grade level and work together in the writers/artists workshop. Students learn from each other as they view exhibitions in classroom galleries and all-school exhibitions. Students have an opportunity to see and use the skills and lenses of artists, writers, and scientists.

The following connections occur across the curriculum when art and writing are partners:

- Pictures take on new significance.
- Artwork has a new power as a form of expression.
- Publishing takes new forms.
- There is more investment in writing.
- A wider range of writing emerges: description, reflection, explanation, poetry, story.
- Pictures are a springboard to writing for reluctant writers.
- There is more art across the curriculum.
- Students improve their ability to revise, speak, listen, and observe.
- There is more analytical, critical, complex thinking.
- Subject areas are naturally integrated.
- There are new collaborations between teachers and with students.

Forming Partnerships

Learning and teaching are no longer isolated. Students bring their stories to art and their pictures to the classroom. A student opening his journal to share in the art room says, "I haven't written about my picture yet." Students expect what we expect, that both writing and art are important in helping us express ourselves.

The focus for the classroom teacher is teaching writing. Pictures help us do that. We learn from our students, and share what we learn with other classes and with each other. The learning community we strive to achieve—in our classrooms and in our schools—is broadened.

Just as I ask a third-grade class, "Does anyone want to share?," the door of the art room opens and Robert, a first grader, walks in.

"I want you to see this. I think it is a surprise," he says as he hands me a picture he has made in his classroom writers workshop. I hold up his blurry watercolor of a tiger standing on a "line" of green grass against a blue sky, but Robert seems annoyed. "Ms. Ernst, not the picture. It is the writing that is a surprise!" I immediately turn over the picture to read aloud the writing stapled to the back: "Today I made a picture of a tiger and I mixed all of the colors. The wise, sly tiger sneaks through the brown, dry reeds. The sun burns through the dry reeds as the afternoon passes." Robert's pride in his surprise is confirmed when a third grader responds, "That's something a fourth grader would write!"

The partnership between writing and art goes beyond the artists workshop. In the classroom there is a clear expectation that writing is required and that improved writing is the focus. When teachers work collaboratively, they create structures to make new connections happen. They find ways for students to be successful writers by setting a time when students must write, establishing

annie

"This is my first poem"
I never made a poem befo"

Annie brought her poem from writers workshop
so she could do a picture to go with it.
About her favorite color blue. This is the
class — I just asked what would happen
if next year we had artists workshop, writers
workshop together Charlie said I'd write
first to see what pictures to make. Cody
said "we sort of did that today!!"

deadlines for publishing and requiring student sharing. With art as a natural and powerful means of observation and expression, with an awareness that writers need images to write with clarity and purpose, it follows that making art part of the writers workshop and the rest of the curriculum improves writing and learning.

Liz begins a picture in the artists workshop, Canadian geese flying across the moon floating in a blurry purple-and-blue sky, and continues the work of art in writers workshop, crafting a poem:

THE FALL MOON

The fall moon
Shimmers on a gaggle of geese
The sky paints a perfect picture
The geese honk
"To the Moon, to the Light,
to the Stars, to the Bright!"
As the night grows older
The geese land,
One by one,
And the goose moon
Fades into the dawn.

Students help us see the connection between art and writing in many ways. The experience I provide in art expands when students take a picture into the classroom and use it to craft a poem. Children learn that in school, as in life, subjects overlap and need each other. As students learn skills for living, their pictures and words change the way teachers and I look at the fall moon, rain on the field, a tornado, dawn.

A poem, a picture—each possible because of the other. The partnership between art and writing and between the practice and the beliefs of teachers pushes us to see new and important links between disciplines and form partnerships with one another and with parents to make and sustain necessary changes. We need to make this link part of the learning history—and the future—of the children we teach.

Experience for Yourself

□ Make a picture and write about it. Use one of the leads suggested in this chapter.
□ At the end of an activity in any subject, ask your students to write about what they learned or discovered. Give them specific directions.

- What are the ways in which students use writing in your classroom?
- What are the ways in which you learn what your students think learning means?
- Make a picture of the place you grew up, a memory of your childhood, or a place you have visited. Spend time with the picture. Write the memory.
- Recall an image—something in your backyard, on your way to work. Let the picture settle clearly in your mind's eye. Write that image, using language that paints a picture on the page.

6

Opening the Doors to Change

Today I was copying the snowman that Mrs. Cirino made. His scarf looked like the wind was blowing. I found this picture on the teachers' learning board. There are other pictures there done by moms and teachers.

—Megan, age 7

In order to connect writing and art beyond the artists workshop, teachers must talk together about what they do in their classroom and parents must understand and support what goes on there. Everyone must feel safe enough with the process of change to risk making things better—introduce new structures that extend children's means of expression, make assessment more comprehensive, integrate the curriculum in new ways, develop higher expectations.

Change begins with a teacher and an idea. It grows and is sustained when it is propelled by the experience and inquiry of many teachers. It is fully realized when parents add their voices and become partners in the process. When we open the doors of our classrooms, we change the ways in which we learn and teach.

The Door of Information

We can inform others about our ideas in many ways. We need to help parents and teachers understand how and why learning can be different from when they went to school.

At the beginning of each school year, I invite parents to a meeting in which I explain the artists workshop and the ways classroom teachers and I work together to benefit their children. I show examples of children's art and writing and list the ways parents can support the work we do in the artists workshop and beyond:

- Volunteer to organize materials in the classroom and help children as they work.
- Experience art and writing as part of their own literacy.
- Talk with their children about their art and writing.
- Offer their own learning as a model.
- Volunteer to put up exhibitions of children's work.
- Attend the exhibitions.
- Share their expertise: conduct a minilesson, do an artist's share.
- Accompany a teacher to a professional development workshop.
- Take visitors on tours of the school and help them understand what they see.
- Ask questions.
- Advocate for excellence: write a letter to the principal or the board of education; tell others in the community about the good job the school is doing.

I describe the routine in the artists workshop, emphasize the importance of stopping to read the easel, explain how reading and writing are essential in art, invite visitors into the workshop, offer students' portfolios for review. I open the door to collaboration.

Throughout the year, brief articles in the weekly PTA newsletter explaining the concept of choice, discussing the uses of literature and art, and announcing portfolio reviews or all-school exhibitions keep parents aware of what is going on instead of leaving them to question what they do not understand. Knowledge creates a foundation for the acceptance of change.

Sending home portfolios of student work informs parents about what their children are doing and why. My letter accompanying the portfolio explains the process of the artists workshop. As parents review the work with their child, they learn that every picture tells a story and has meaning, that ideas can be generated by artists, authors, and other children, that their child is developing confidence in self-expression. The child's voice is a powerful conduit of information. (For a more detailed look at portfolio review, see Chapter 11.)

All-school exhibitions inform the entire school community. They are spaces for learning and teaching. Signs explain how children use sketch journals, how artist's share teaches listening and speaking skills. Pages from artist's notebooks and sketch journals are displayed next to an explanation that they are unedited drafts of thinking. It is important to inform the audience that the exhibition shows both work in process and final product. When children are seated on the floors in the hallways, sketching and writing about the pictures, everyone can observe the skills and enthusiasm children learn in the artists workshop.

The Door of Observation

I take my sketch journal into teachers' classrooms, observing with the lens of an art teacher, wondering how to connect art with the curriculum, raising questions to help me become a better teacher. Watching Darcy Hicks conduct a minilesson on her expectations for writing helps me rethink my own expectations for students in the artists workshop. I draw first graders in Mary Sue Welch's room as they work on pictures in her writers workshop. I wonder if they have more investment in these pictures, which are connected to their stories and their classroom teacher, than in the pictures they make in the art room. As Peter von Euler's fourth graders draw a simple machine to help them understand how it works, then write about the machine using the vocabulary they've learned, I begin to see the ways in which art and writing impact learning in science.

Classroom teachers expand their learning by visiting the artists workshop. Liz Olbrych sits in a chair at the edge of the rug and takes notes as one of her students shares her work; she receives a more complete picture of her student's learning. Lynn Gehr listens to the meeting I have with her second graders about how to collect ideas for leads, and uses what she learns when her students return to the classroom. Dawn Damiani's visits to the art room help her consider the parallel between visual images that inspire pictures and word images that inspire writing.

Structures to make art part of the writers workshop emerged from the observations we made in each other's classrooms. This began as a pilot project with one teacher from first to forth grades and I collaborating. Our inquiry, regular meetings, sharing questions and problems helped each of us plan for our own grade and classroom. Sharing our learning in The Community of Teachers Learning encouraged others to learn from our small but important beginning pilot project. The knowledge we gained helped others sketch their own plan for connecting art to their writers workshops. Since that first year the connections have grown to include most teachers and classrooms in the school.

Learning from one another through observation means that the children and their work are at the center of how our classrooms change. Change begins with personal observations and experiences and develops as teachers meet to discuss their learning and translate these observations into action.

The Door of Conversation

Change builds when teachers meet and talk together. The teachers at our school meet regularly in a study group—A Community of Teachers Learning. These meetings spread ideas, increase inquiry and collaboration, and propel change in the school. Each teacher brings her observations, his knowledge and questions,

Did observations of Fast Plants → stood to Pledge of the Flag →

writing in observation journals

"Take out your observation journals.
Write the date April 1.
These are your choices for
writing. (see previous page).

By this time of the year —
things are routine, in place,
and the expectations are here.
Write in silence, listen, use
writing to think, to even
move into the
day. I see
connections
everywhere.
And this
writing will
help me make sense.
Peter took home ½
of the observation
journals of his students
to read over the
weekend. He passed
those back while
the others took
theirs out of ~~their~~ their
desks.

Expectation:
Bring it to school
everyday. I will
read it and not
only respond
but it will give me
new ideas for teaching

Glenn and Jack. Morning Exercises

and by sharing them, begins to feel safe enough to take risks, experiment, and raise new questions.

Our biweekly meetings focus on our practice as teachers—what we question, observe, do well, and want to do better; how we can become better observers; and how children can inform what we do. One person's inquiry—student choice in the art room, drawing as a tool of observation, links between picture making and writing—informs the practice and inquiry of the others. We begin each year by asking, *What do you wonder about in your teaching?* Some recent questions include:

How can I connect my reading program with writing?

How can I develop a stronger classroom community?

How can I connect my assessment of my special education students to the work in the classroom more effectively?

How can I find the time to reflect on my teaching of music?

How can I balance teaching and caring for two small children at home?

The group's purpose is revised to reflect its changing membership. The meetings are a way to mentor and support new teachers and stimulate veteran teachers. The conversation at any meeting propels our questions and excitement about teaching and learning. A Community of Teachers Learning is not intended to create a separate group within the school but to add to the knowledge and community of everyone in the school. Brief minutes of each meeting are distributed to the entire faculty.

Our two-hour, after-school meetings have an agenda; this gives us some structure and helps keep the conversatons positive and productive. We don't avoid difficult issues, but keep an eye on solutions instead of just voicing complaints. Our agenda looks like this:

- Food and conversation.
- Set date for next meeting; identify facilitators and hosts.
- Learning: discuss professional literature (an article, a chapter from a book); share information from a recent conference; make an informal presentation; share student work.
- Writing: what do you wonder about what we've just discussed? what happened in your classroom in the last two weeks that was exciting or troubling? which student is particularly in your thoughts today?
- Sharing: discuss what each person wrote.

The writing portion of the meeting gives each participant time to think about his or her classroom—a student who is struggling, a lesson that went well, a question he or she has about what went on. It focuses us on the personal and

Writing at C.O.T.L. —
The cold room is finally quiet and
we write. I am struck by how
much teaching or leading adults
is like doing same for kids.
Once the group is brought to ~~order~~
and writing is announced)   it's the
there is increased volume in talk —
rehearsal everyone needs before they write.

And so C.O.T.L. I really believe it has worked
to develop a Community but is it Teacher's Learning?
I guess my idea is to make this an even

keeps us from complaining about issues that are too big for us to solve. Our own classroom, our own teaching and learning, are where we can make a difference.

Our writing propels our discussion. When one teacher—the media specialist, a kindergarten teacher, a fourth-grade teacher—reads what she has written, responses from the rest of the group broaden the focus of the conversation: choice in the curriculum, teaching writing and spelling, parent conferences, teaching math, using sketch journals across the curriculum, involving parents in a positive way, establishing classroom routines, alternative scheduling.

The Door of Experience

Parents and teachers learn from their own experiences in the artists workshop. A parent helping with a museum field trip learns when she hears children talk about works and artists they recognize and decide which works to draw and write about. She learns when she compares this field trip with her own experience as a student: never having gone to a museum; taking a course in which the teacher told her what to see when she looked at a particular painting and then tested her later to see whether she could parrot back what she had been told.

A parent asks, "Why will they draw at the museum?," and I realize again that a process familair to my students is not part of the history of their parents. My answer educates, reemphasizes what I believe: "Drawing helps them see and think about the works." Questions are not a threat but an opening to understanding how things can be different.

Parents and teachers learn firsthand in the artists workshop. When Kerry Cooper volunteers once a week to help keep the artists workshop organized, she also learns about my intention to bring art into literacy. She watches children participate in artist's share and sees evidence that they are acquiring skills in listening and speaking. She learns as she watches children focus seriously and authentically on their own ideas.

Barbara Marquette wants to attempt a picture of her own but admits she doesn't have an idea and doesn't know what to use, so third grader Sally takes her on a tour of the room and explains that copying is a legitimate way to get started. The library of ideas takes on a new meaning. Fourth grader Jennifer is understanding when Vicki Sloat is afraid to begin her picture: "She's afraid it won't turn out. I used to feel that way about using a black pen. I thought I would be terrible at it."

The Door of Community

Pictures by teachers and parents—a woodland scene copied from a picture book, a white egret in a grassy marsh, a memory of summer in Rhode Island— are pinned to the bulletin board headed *Teachers and Parents Are Learners Too*.

Mrs.
Sloat and
Jennifer

Jennifer answered – She's afraid it won't turn out.
I want to see what the crayons do without you.

I felt that way before I started to use the
black pen. I thought I would be Terrible at it.

I was always kept a journal – always doodled in
it – always draw nature.

Painting class: Teacher only painted white.
In elementary – Bad memories – not doing it right.
Being told I wasn't an artist, my sister was

Students copy a picture they see there, carry it to the creator of the original, and say, "You inspired my work today." The adults understand, because the children's work propelled and inspired *them!*

The work on the bulletin board, the presence of teachers and parents in the workshop, show children that adults are still learning and that what we are teaching them is important for a lifetime. Students mentoring adults expands everyone's learning. Adults learn firsthand what it feels like to have someone notice their work, to be too scared to begin, to experience the relief when someone shows you how to start or says, "I know how you feel."

Experiences like these connect students, teachers, and parents in new ways. We are no longer teaching just the students in our individual classrooms but all the children in the school. We sketch our own plans for ways that art and writing connect as a result of own experiences—collaboration, classroom visits, observation, making art.

We link our expectations and structures in the process. We share the belief that art is a form of expression and is a springboard to thinking and writing. We know that reading and looking at art are important ways to begin the writers workshop. We know how important it is for students to share with one another—in their own classroom and in other classrooms—and that choice in the classroom means responsibility, not unstructured freedom. We understand that sketch journals link what children and teachers do in the art room and in the classroom and broaden our assessments. When we share our observations with one another, we develop more comprehensive pictures of our students' progress.

The Door of Risk

Teachers together can begin to step toward change naturally—growing from their own learning experiences. Change is not so frightening. When Kristi Blob and Dawn Damiani notice a difference in their second graders—Kristi's are doing well using sketch journals for observation and Dawn's are doing well writing descriptively about pictures—they decide to switch classes to find out why. One week later they understand that it is not the class or the children that are different but their own expertise and style of teaching.

Change occurs when people no longer feel isolated, when they are willing to raise questions, know they will not be judged but joined by a colleageue in finding answers.

Finding Your Public Voice

When teachers form their own questions and seek their own answers, teaching becomes an exciting intellectual experience. When one teacher's questions and

Mary Sue takes time
between 11 – 11:30
to

Mary Sue:
"Yesterday
in writing
workshop
I asked
them
to try
something
new —
that was
very
difficult

Also this
is the last
day for
cartoon
characters
& Sonic"

IW
Mary Sue Welch

Timothy —
The hole in the tree is
on the other side
when someone was
touching
"This is a work of art!"

at the
beginning
of writers'
workshop

Julie:
The Wrinkled Rainbow

Anna: "It doesn't really
look like a
rainbow because it has
all these dots on it."

Mary Sue
is
engaged
and pushes
them to try new things
— Sue is definitely involved in
writing & science.

David's comments
always come from
someone else's ideas

the hedgehog

"Do you want to
read your
reflection?"
"It's a poem!"
(Jesse).

knowledge drive change in a classroom, other teachers begin to feel confident to speak publicly about what they know. They find their public voice.

Darcy Hicks teaches us to help students revise by encouraging them to resee the ideas in their pictures. Peter von Euler helps us see how assignments in drawing and writing can lead students to become more astute observers and questioners in science. Dawn Damiani extends our knowledge of ways to connect the experiences of picture making with imagery in literature and writing.

Talking together in the context of issues such as choice or expectation in writing brings about a natural, lasting, powerful change. Our conversations link us with teachers at our grade level, at other grade levels, in the next town, across the country. They extend our interest in observing and learning from one other and in continuing to expand ideas for educating parents and children. They help teachers find their public voice and let their good ideas bring change in the school. They place our work in the context of the children and ensure that when change occurs in school it will come from what we know, think, observe, and reflect in connection with one another.

In turn, the authority of the teacher changes. Liz Olbrych finds structures that establish parents as partners in her classroom. She teaches them what she expects and asks them to work within the limits she defines. Linda Stern shows us that sometimes the most important parent partners are those who do not have children in the classroom, because they can more effectively focus on the learning and teaching of all. Teachers are in charge of the learning and teaching in their classroom and constantly seek to improve both. Their job includes educating parents and welcoming their questions.

We use our public voices to write locally, share professionally, and speak about the work of children. We continue to find new ways for children to say what they mean, express themselves, find *their* public voice, and establish their important place in teaching and learning.

Changing, Growing

Together we continue to redefine "integrating the curriculum." Classroom teachers no longer ask me to teach Egyptian art during that unit of study; rather, we work at literacy together, each using his or her ideas and expertise to broaden the areas of expression available to our students.

Students no longer wonder why the art teacher is in their classroom to lead writing or observe a science lesson or why their classroom teacher is making a picture in art class. As teachers keep sketch journals, carry them into other classrooms, use them to observe and question, children see us all as their teachers. Our model of learning together opens the door for them to teach minilessons to other classes, describe what they did in class last year as a way to add to the learning in their current classroom, or keep sketch journals of their own.

Linking art and writing in the artists workshop is only a beginning. When I open the door for others to learn, resee, and rethink an idea and translate it into their own classroom or life, the idea takes hold. Real change occurs and endures.

Experience for Yourself

- Who is the colleague with whom you collaborate, to whom you tell your teaching stories, with whom you wonder about your successes and failures? Write about your relationship with this person.
- Read a brief article with a colleague. Respond to it in writing, then discuss your response.
- What have you learned from your colleagues? Make a list.
- Write for twenty minutes about what you wonder about in your teaching and learning.
- Capture in words a student, a lesson, or a moment in the day. Write it so that your imagined audience can see what you saw, feel what you felt.
- Make a list of ways that parents could be of help in your classroom. What do you need to do to make that happen?
- Observe a colleague. Use your sketch journal to draw and write what you see. What ideas does this give you for your own classroom?

7

The Student Sketch Journal: Connecting Learning and Teaching

Drawing helps me record memories. In science we record observations by sketching. In writers workshop I draw to observe and that helps me write. . . . I think that drawing leads me to passages of writing, and writing and art put together equal one thought, one observation, one expression. Art is made to give an artist a closer look.

—Maggie, age 9

The sketch journal does not make the connection between art and writing happen, it is the result of that connection. Teachers collaborating with one another to link art and learning keep sketch journals in order to experience the link for themselves. They use their sketch journals as a guide to how they ask students to use theirs. Teachers discover ways to use sketch journals in their classroom to connect art and writing to subjects in the curriculum. Ways of using sketch journals differ from grade to grade, from teacher to teacher, and from year to year.

Take notes in your own sketch journal as you listen to students describe the writing and drawing they did for an assignment in the classroom. Listen to the clarity of their voices, look at how the journal pages reveal the uniqueness of each child, how together the drawings and writing reveal why their sketch journals are important to them, to the curriculum, and to learning in and out of school.

In Their Own Voice

Classroom teachers and I work together to prepare students before handing out sketch journals each year: we make our expectations for using them clear and find ways that they can become integral to the classroom curriculum.

When Courtney receives her new fourth grade sketch journal—even after keeping one since first grade—she writes that she feels special and free. "I look at myself included in a big circle with all of the official journal writers. I feel excited and calm. It makes me feel good to know that I have a journal."

Danielle sits in a chair at the edge of the rug in the artists workshop, ready to share the first page of her sketch journal with her class and me. She received it the day before in her classroom. My sketch journal, open and ready, tells the class I need their answers to my questions about how a sketch journal helps them, how they use it, what it shows about them.

"I am eight years old," Danielle says. "I plan to use my sketch journal to write my feelings and write what I did. On the first page I copied a picture from a book."

Other students hold open a page of their journal and give their classmates and me a glimpse inside.

"I copied from an art card. I just liked the lion. I wrote a story about it."

"I was looking at a book and it gave me an idea because we are studying the ocean. I drew the ocean."

"This is a memory of the first time my cat climbed a tree. That is why I made the picture."

Sometimes teachers introduce the sketch journal in the classroom, other times a classroom teacher and I introduce it together. Either way it is a collaboration, because it is connected to the ideas of the artists workshop—choice, art, literature, drawing, writing—and to the work and learning in the classroom. It is part of the classroom routine, part of the student's daily thinking and learning. It builds another bridge between art and the classroom, between art and learning.

Expectations

The general structure and expectation are the same from grade to grade or teacher to teacher—date the entries, number the pages, use it to draw, write, think, notice, and wonder.

Rosie takes notes on the first page of her journal as her teacher and I introduce sketch journals to her fourth-grade class. It is a list of tips about using it:

Draw and write everyday

Make the first page special

Mistakes okay

Copying okay

Learn by keeping and reading back over the journal

Appreciate the journal

Think about things

Students anticipate getting sketch journals in the first months of the school year. Teachers prepare their class by first developing a sense of community—

Sharing
Sketch
Journals
2 M

"I am 8 years old."

I plan to use it
to write my
feelings and
write what I
did.

First page
copied
from a
book.

First page
copied from an
art card —
just liked the lion

"I wrote a story"

Samantha —
I was looking
at "I Am an Ocean." Gave
me an idea because we are
studying the ocean.

Homework
How did it feel
when you got
your sketch journal.

Preston: This is a memory of the first time
my cat climbed a tree.
That's why I made the picture.

writing, talking, and listening together—and encouraging the habit of writing about and finding meaning in their pictures. The students are familiar with writing to think and drawing to observe.

We make very clear that the journal is part of the students' schoolwork: they will be guided in how and when to use it; assignments will be given; and it will be read by the teachers and shared in other ways. A sketch journal provides students with a new lens for learning and gives their teachers new and unique glimpses into the students and what they learn. The sketch journal travels with the students to the artists workshop, on field trips, to museums, and on vacations. Each teacher determines where in the classroom they will be stored and if and when children will take them home.

Getting a sketch journal is always presented as a privilege; as Rosie noted, it is important always to appreciate the journal.

A class of first graders prepares for getting their journals by listening to a panel of second graders discuss how they use theirs. Third graders anticipate getting a new journal to provide them with a new start; they reflect on how they used it the year before. Early in third grade, Marc tells his teacher he needs his new journal because it is the way he keeps his thoughts organized. In it, he writes down quotes from artists and sketches things he observes; both help him move on to detailed written observations.

Asking third and fourth graders to write about their goals and plans for using their sketch journal frames their anticipation. Fourth graders write:

I'm going to try to write for every picture, not make it a whole jungle of pictures.

I will keep drawing until I get things right.

Most of the time when I am really satisfied it is because the pictures and the writing are both good. I enjoy pictures more than writing but this year I want to make that equal.

Connection, preparation, and anticipation are essential to establishing high expectations.

The Front Page

The room is silent as a class of fourth graders begin work on the first page of their sketch journal. Atsuko writes, "This is the day I got my new eyes. This is the day I become an observer. My heart started to pound." Francesca and Sarah copy comments from the assignment the class did before receiving their journal: "Helps me let out my ideas." "I knew I could capture my thoughts." "I know I can look back." "It will hold things important." "It is a symbol of my imagination." "Every little picture is important."

Steven waits to do his first page and draws a sailboat on the second page. "I want to practice first to improve," he tells me. "A sailboat was the first thing that came to my mind. I love the thought of them. There is a motorboat skimming in the distance, making the water break here." The picture gives presence to the poetry of his words.

David remembers being on Lake Michigan last summer. Rebecca kneels on the floor, her sketch journal propped on one leg, and draws a small section of the art room. She tells me, "I focus on one thing and I just keep going."

These students have intention and focus as they begin their sketch journals. They take in what they see, remember, or love. Christopher whispers, "It helps my creative part melt out of me and spill onto the paper. It lets my imagination go wild." Sketch journals help make room in the curriculum for a child's imagination.

Inside and Outside the Classroom

Younger students use sketch journals to observe things they see in the classroom, outside, on a field trip, or in their imagination.

First graders get sketch journals and take them on field trips to the zoo and the farm. Their sketches of cows and pigs and monkeys are a record of their visit and a way to help them pay attention when looking.

A student's sketch of the daffodils blooming in the school yard leads her to write, "The daffodils are swaying. The daffodils are bright yellow. It seems like they are giggling." Another draws the shadow a vase of daffodils casts on the rug in her first-grade classroom. Sketch journals help students slow down, notice details inside and look closely outside.

Second grader Matthew draws what he sees as he lies on his stomach face to face with the daffodils, stone wall in the background, house and flag across the street. His observation and experience lead to writing about his feelings: "Today I was copying some daffodils. I felt that I was alone out in the wilderness with only my sketchbook and my pencil, just drawing away at my surroundings. They were so beautiful that I decided to draw them." When students make drawing and observing part of their regular school experience, they develop skills in drawing, in paying attention, and in putting their feelings into words.

Sharing Learning from the Classroom

In many cases, sketch journals replace writer's notebooks and link the work in the classroom to the art room. Students carry them in, meet me on the rug, and use them to share their writing, thinking, and observations.

Gaby clutches her sketch journal as she sits in the chair by the rug, ready to share. She has entered the room ahead of her class and declared, "I need to

Christina

Frank lying on the grass
drawing the daffodils.

Tomani

"Where should I start?" as she sits ready
to draw the crab apple tree.

Anthony.

With 35 outside. The dynamic of this class is incredible
all individuals — no let's work as a team
and as the year has gone on it is exagerated.
By the time I talked, etc. we came out at 12:00.

share." It is the day after a ten-day vacation from school, and I have been thinking that perhaps students will come to art without any ideas.

Gaby's pencil drawing of the curtains at her bedroom window is hard to "read," but it is clear that she needs to share more than a picture. "I looked out the window and saw a rock," she tells us. "I thought about the sunset from where I used to live in New York City, so I drew a sunset, then a sun. And after that I wrote. I thought it might give you an idea for your own writing." Then she reads from her sketch journal. "'As I sit here in bed, drawing away, I just can't stop. I never found the secret to drawing until I really concentrated on what I was sketching. All of my pictures look like nothing compared to what I'm drawing now.'" She looks up and addresses us directly again. "As an artist I have changed. Maybe I gave you a tip, or maybe not. If you concentrate really hard, your pencil might take you far away."

Gaby notices a window, moves on to a memory, and comes to an understanding. Her sketch journal helps her link thinking, art, writing, and meaning in very natural ways. It leads her to concentrate and uncover secrets—her own learning discoveries—with such force that she must share them with her classmates. Gaby and her sketch journal are the real teachers today.

Other students share entries made on field trips. Ali shows the page on which she has drawn a spider crab she saw at the beach and written a poem in the voice of the crab.

When students carry their sketch journals to the art room and share pieces like these, I find out what they are studying in the classroom, they realize that I am interested in their stories as well as their pictures, and I get ideas about how I can connect what goes on in art to the classroom. It is natural and authentic integration of curriculum. Sketch journals are a tool by which students can look and learn with the lens of an artist wherever they are.

Connecting Art and the Classroom

Sketch journals capture students' learning history. When they are carried from classroom to artists workshop and back again, that history includes work in all the disciplines. Art is not separate, on the margin, but part of the day, the life, the mind.

Students keep their sketch journals handy as they work in the artists workshop; they take notes on their process. Nicole writes, "I think I should spend more time on my picture." When Elizabeth has trouble sculpting a duck out of clay, Justin opens his journal to a sketch he had done of a mallard duck to help her visualize it. Sketch journals are a tool by which to examine the process of learning and a way in which students mentor one another.

Classroom teachers ask their students to write before going to the art room, to plan what they will do there, to think before they work. "Today I plan to try something new . . . do a clay record . . . finish my collage . . . look for an idea. . . ."

I ask students to write in their sketch journals at the end of art period, and some classroom teachers provide silent writing time after art period as well. Sketch journals help students share their classroom learning with me and provide a place in which teachers can ask students to really think about their learning in art. These connections help us better understand our students and push our students to new understanding as they spend time with their picture and their writing.

Connecting the Beginning to the End

Claire takes her collage to her classroom in order to write about it. Two small green squares of tissue paper float in the center of a large piece of white paper. On one square is a blue circle—a pond—with tiny pieces of paper—flowers—next to it. On the other green square is a pink house.

Claire's collage is her memory of a visit to her cousin's farm. Her writing takes us inside that tiny pink house, describes everyone and everything going on there. The little blue circle of a pond comes to life as she writes about going to the pond to pick flowers—"daisies, daffodils, roses, tulips, indigos, and more." The green squares are leaves. "We put them in a large green leaf that is large enough to fit both of our hands in." Claire moves from her memory to explain the title she has given it. "I named my picture 'A World of Art' because art can be many things, such as a memory, writing, a picture, imagination, and words. Whenever I have a day without art, I don't seem to be as happy as normal."

Claire has been thinking of a poem for which she has the beginning but no ending. Talking to the paper as though it is her audience, she writes, "I'll tell you a little of the beginning," and goes on to draft her poem:

> A day without art is like a day without sunshine.
> Birds don't sing, horses don't nay, the flowers go away.
> Imagination has died.
> I sit on my window seat with a pad of paper and pen.
> I look out. The world is dark and dull, no light.
> No words to be spoken in my head, dancing, twirling,
> itching to be put down on paper.
> A day without art and imagination
> is a day without sunshine.

Then she writes, "I just figured out my ending while I was writing!"

Sustained silent writing for thirty minutes in the classroom about her work in art has led Claire to a discovery. She needs time to reflect and practice her thinking. She has two teachers who are connected—both are her audience and both believe in pictures as an expression of meaning and a form of expressing ideas. When Claire carries her art and her sketch journal between the classroom and the artists workshop, she connects what she learns in both places, connects her picture to her thinking to her writing. She connects beginnings with endings and expands her learning.

With sketch journals as part of the classroom and artists workshop routine, there need never be a day without art, a world without a place in which to express, discover, observe, and wonder in pictures and words.

A Closer Look: Observation Journals

The fourth-grade teachers in our school call the sketch journals observation journals, because they want their students to focus on drawing and writing about things they observe. They want to connect the journal to science and literature.

Observation journals began in Peter von Euler's fourth-grade classroom as he wrote and drew in his own journal and used what he found there as leads for minilessons. Each year his experience, the experience of other fourth-grade teachers who have learned from him, and the experiences of their students reveal more possibilities for using sketch journals in many areas of the curriculum. Specific journal assignments in science, reading, and writing, and guidance in carrying them out, helps increase the value of journals to students and to teachers as a mirror of student progress.

Peak over the shoulders of Peter's fourth graders as they move silently from desk to desk, looking at and reading observation journals open to last night's homework assignment, in which Peter asked them to draw something in their room at home, something that had meaning, held a memory. He urged them to draw to explore the object and to let the drawing lead them to the memory, to the writing: "I want them to write until they make connections." Spending time looking at an object while drawing it allows ideas, memories, thoughts to surface.

Anna's writing fills the edges of the page next to the drawing of her desk. "I noticed that the desk size doesn't fit my lamp in the picture." Drawing helps students observe the details, see what they often take for granted. Their skills in critiquing develop as they use the pages in their journals for studies, sketches, thought.

Frisk has drawn a simple name plaque in his room. The drawing helps him see what he looked at. "I notice I put this plaque all by itself in the room. I never noticed how bare it is in this part of the room. The plaque gives me memories of when I did things that were fun. I got it in first grade."

leads

When you began what
did you notice. As
you continued
drawing and writing –
describe details.

What do memory
is in this thing
you drew.
Try to capture the
moment of the
memory in
words.

What did
you feel like
or think about.

Paying attention to objects helps a student see his own history, meaning, and uniqueness. David writes, "I picked this part of my room because this part really feels like me. The poster tells that I am Chinese."

Assignments like these produce writing with voice and provide ideas to return to for extended writing topics. The page in Ann's journal shows her dolls and leads her to a memory of playing with them. Her classmates notice how her writing brings her memory to life and gives them ideas for their next observation. Kristen's sketch of a painting, a "copy of a van Gogh," shows that she makes the work of artists part of her repertoire at home as well as school. Kelsey's drawing of a music box prompts her to remember how she would always sneak into her older sister's room to listen to her music box. "Now I have to worry about my little brother listening to mine. It is a small world."

Assignments like this make the small things big, help reveal meaning, moments, memories, that give each student's life an imprint, a uniqueness. Other assignments fourth-grade teachers give their students include:

- Draw something that you observe and write about it.
- Draw it again from a different perspective.
- Draw something that holds a memory.
- Draw something you observe and write the questions that occur as you look.

The expectation is clear that when the students draw their observation, they will write one as well. Peter von Euler says that reading his students' journals is "like shining a light into a teaming cave." The journals connect students to their world and to one another. They help students look close up, back away and see things anew, notice things they have overlooked, go inside and realize meaning and memories. And since their journals are their own, they see things and say things in their own way, in their own words, in their authentic voice.

Conversations with Artists, Writers, Scientists

When illustrators and authors come to our school, they bring their works in progress, their finished pieces, and their sketch journals. Students sit in the audience—in the classroom or library or art room—with their own sketch journals open, drawing and taking notes.

Hardie Gramatky's daughter shows us that he wrote much more than he drew. Writing of a time when he was sad helped him capture the feeling of sadness on Little Toot's face.

When Lynne Reiser holds up her sketch journal—which is identical to the one the fourth graders use—an important link is made between what these students do and the real world of artists and writers. As she turns the pages of her journal, filled with sketches of feet she drew at the beach, she tells how her idea for a counting book featuring the feet of different animals evolved. She explains that her drawing is a link to her knowledge as a biologist, scientist, and doctor.

Cat Bowman-Smith explains how her sketch journal is a tool in her research. Capturing the essence of places she visits helps her draw the settings of the books she illustrates.

When each professional finishes speaking, the students raise their hands to ask questions. *Do you ever copy? What happens when you make a mistake? Do you ever tear out a page from your sketch journal?* Their questions come from their own curiosity and are grounded in their experience in keeping a sketch journal.

Then they are eager to share how their sketch journal helps them in their learning and work. Glenn shows how a drawing helps him realize the incredible size of a butterfly's wings compared with its body. Brittany explains that her daily drawings in a science unit on embryology help her understand and remember the life cycle of chicks. Caitlyn shows a sketch of a flower she did on a field trip and tells us that it became a study for a picture she made for an exhibition. Sydney explains that drawing and writing help her "explore the plant more" in a unit on the growth of a plant from tiny sprout to full maturity in thirty days. Drake shows a picture of a bat: "I felt like the bat was holding onto me. I tried to draw without lifting my pen." Maggie shows a design for her electrical project and says that the drawing helped her realize the project was too complicated to carry out. Ursula shows a page on which she has drawn many details in a flower she observed. "I had more to say after I had closely observed it," she explains. Tyler says, "My head was basically in the flower when I sketched it." His drawing was up close, his writing poetic.

Students use their own sketch journals in the same way artists, writers, and scientists use theirs. Lynne Reiser reminds the students that scientists must prove that they saw something and that they understand it. The students show Lynne that their sketch journal helps them do that. After Antonio Frasconi makes his presentation, students line up to have him autograph their sketch journals. The line moves slowly, because they are eager to share pages from the journals they hand to him. He says later, "You can see their spontaneity, their minds working. When adults see a white piece of paper they are afraid. These students are not."

Taking It All In

On a field trip to the nature center fourth graders use their sketch journal to see and listen. They sketch the preserved owls, herons, and hawks. In a room where silence is required, looking and thinking encouraged, the line of pens and pencils discovers the backward direction of a heron's knee, the slow blink of an owl's eye, the way a plant spreads as it branches out, the size of a butterfly's wings.

Taking the path through the woods, crossing a bridge over the bog, they stop to sketch to see, they write to listen. They draw the leaf of a huge fern, the branch of a tree, a huge root bulging from the bog. They notice "the reflections on the bog," "the caterpillars making a web," "a bird flying away," "how the roots of the trees stand out of the water," that "where the water is blurry the reflections of the trees don't move."

A visitor with us that day is unpracticed in drawing and writing to observe. She has great difficulty because she only sees the whole bog, doesn't know where to begin, how to fit it onto the page. Sketch journals give students practice focusing on the details.

Wally announces, "I'm going to bring my sketch journal on a camp-out by a lake so I can wake up early in the morning and sketch the mist." Keeping a sketch journal leads students to see their surroundings differently, anticipate taking them in, capturing them on a page.

At the Museum of Natural History students look at the pages from Leonardo da Vinci's notebook. Their sketch journals in their hands are their eyes, their ears, their minds thinking. Viewing the documentary that accompanies the exhibit, they take notes about how observations in nature led Leonardo to questions, wondering, and knowledge. They learn how his observations in science fed into his work as an artist. They copy passages from his pages onto their own. They draw the inventions that the museum has created based on the sketches from Leonardo's journal. We learn that he was an artist, a scientist, a philosopher. For him, learning wasn't filled with disconnection but with connection. Students make connections of their own.

Experience for Yourself

- Do a contour drawing of an object. Write what you noticed about the object.
- Draw every day for one week. Write why you selected the object, what you noticed about your drawing each time, and the process involved in doing it. What did you think about or notice each day?
- Select an object and draw it several times, each time from a different perspective. Write down what you noticed about the object, yourself, or the drawing after doing each one.
- Find something that "holds a memory"—a photograph, a painting, a gift—and draw it. Write about the memory.

- Do a picture three times, each time using a different medium. How did the picture change? What did you notice about repeating a picture several times?
- Draw an object to help you understand how it works (a toaster, lightbulb, music box). Write down how you think it works.
- Draw the place in which you grew up or a moment that you remember from your childhood. Write about the place or the moment.
- Draw from memory something you can go see. Then look at the object or place and draw it as you look. Describe the difference or how the drawing helped you look more closely.
- Draw something from nature. Write down what you wonder.
- Draw and write as you listen to a story or a poem.
- Copy a picture. Then write about what you noticed as you drew it.
- Draw and write in your sketch journal as other people are talking or when you watch a video.
- Read back over your sketch journal and make a list of what you notice, what you want to work on, how you have changed.

8

The Language of Writers and Artists

Writing is a way to show your thoughts and fears. I know I have said this before, but I am saying it again. Art is another language. It is a very beautiful language.

—Justin, age 9

I read books by and about writers and artists and keep notes in my sketch journal. I sketch a painting at a museum to help me see and think about it. Sketching helps me read the work, writing leads me to connection. I collect postcards that depict artworks. I copy one, trying to achieve the same thick geometric lines the artist did. I do not copy to reproduce but to gather ideas, learn technique, respond, critique, question, expand my style.

I record the words and ideas of artists and writers: *take time to look; sketchbooks are a constant source of ideas; watercolor studies help a poet capture an observation, see what she might add to the poem.* Just as I read literature to model good writing for children, I read paintings and the ideas of artists to model how we can learn from the artists in our culture.

A classroom teacher asks, "How can I link art with the learning in my classroom when I have no background in art history or in making art?" My answer is the same one I give an art teacher who claims she has no background in teaching writing: Start learning now. Learn through your own experiences, by sitting next to your students, going to museums, reading about the work of artists or authors as part of your preparation for teaching. Read a painting, paint a picture of a poem or piece of writing in order to see it better, or contemplate the words of an artist or writer. Translate their knowledge to help you link art, science, and writing in your classroom.

The language of writers and artists surrounds and informs my classroom. My students and I read literature, go to museums, and look at paintings as we learn together.

My interest in and constant learning from artists and writers is grounded in my role as teacher. The words that I copy into my sketch journal find their way onto posters in my classroom, into my jottings on the blackboard, or into stories I tell my students. They support what we do in the classroom and extend new possibilities.

When Val repeats the same picture of a countryside or Megan keeps copying Monet's painting of a bridge over and over in different materials, I tell her, "Artists do that often, to learn how light changes the object, to express it differently, or to show how they change as an artist." When a teacher in a workshop says to me, "I want to draw a boat, but I don't know how," I lead her to some books with boats and tell her to do what many artists do: learn by copying from others, look to the work of an artist or a writer to add knowledge and technique to her own repertoire. When I pass another teacher in the workshop, I suggest that the line of her drawing has a Matisse-like quality. Linking our classrooms and our lives to the work of artists and writers places what we do in the context of the real world of learning and practice. It makes us want to learn more.

Reading the Pictures

I place van Gogh's *The Houses of Auvers* on the easel. I tell the students to focus on the painting and read it—to think about what they see, colors, shapes, objects, what is happening, what the painting reminds them of, how it makes them feel, what ideas they can gather from it. We pause in silence to really look.

After a minute, students raise their hands. "The trees are blowing in the wind." "There are different colors in the roofs of the houses. I can really see the brush strokes." "It reminds me of Nantucket." "The house is standing alone. It makes me feel like one person—an old person—is in the house." "I like the way he made the sky, blues and whites. It makes it look like there are clouds in the sky."

Students learn to look, listen to one another, and use language to describe what they see; they realize they can respond to a painting. Everyone's comments help each of us look again to find more meaning and go to our own work with new ideas.

Students learn to appreciate art, but this is not "art appreciation." When they learn to look at art and respond to it, they are beginning to build a reason to continue to make art a necessary part of their experience. They discover that meaning in art is accessible, and they develop an interest in the role that art plays in our culture.

Seeing the Words

I read *The Magic Bicycle* by B. Doherty. I tell the class that it is a memory of learning something for the first time, trying over and over until you get it right. "Think about the times when you learned something." As I read, I pause to point out how some pictures are close-ups, others show a bird's-eye view. I explain, "I often look at the pictures and think about what material I would use to copy them." What I choose to read or say grows out of what I notice or think about as I read and learn.

I select books for their beautiful pictures, their imaginative ideas, their stories, the memories they evoke, the styles of artwork they depict, or their poetic or descriptive language. I read to help us settle in, to begin, to focus, to let the word images fill our minds and teach us to pay attention—to see the pictures as I read the words. Reading a picture book helps students listen and leads them to possible ideas for their own work. (At the end of this book is a list of picture books that I use in the artists workshop. The list grows as I continue to learn and teach.)

Copying to Learn

As students make their choices and begin to work, someone invariably asks, "Can I use the book you just read?" Children take that book or one from the "library of ideas" to their work space to copy the pictures. Books are propped up, clipped open as students work on their own pictures. They go through the box of art cards to get ideas for their work. An art reproduction can inspire a picture or a piece of writing. Just as professional artists do, students copy, get ideas for their pictures, learn techniques, use someone else's work as a form of research to learn how to draw a horse, a dragon, or a butterfly.

Cary's layered oil pastel lion, copied from *The Foolish Rabbit's Big Mistake* by Martin and Young, establishes her as an expert, and "that lion" remains a standard for adults and children long after she moves on to middle school. For Katie, copying an owl from *Large as Life* by J. Finzel, working on it for over five weeks, sustains her interest and develops her skill in drawing. Ariel copies Katie but changes the picture in many ways. She writes, "I was inspired by Katie's picture of an owl. I think when I find something that I like, I try to draw it again and again, each time in a different perspective. Last year it was a lion and now it is an owl."

Students "copy" from books, art cards, teachers, and one another and learn to acknowledge the source of their ideas. The notion of copying takes on a new meaning, that of adding to, not taking away from, the original maker. After copying a picture done by a teacher, Tyler writes, "I think copying helps you get

2nd graders sprawl on the rug with clip boards to "copy"

really good ideas. I think copying helps your mind set free. Today I drew a picture of a field. I copied the same color for the water in the stream in the field. In my picture I added very tall grass and a stream."

Often what students write after copying a picture shows how time spent with the picture helps open their imagination. Billy's monthlong effort leads him to write, "Today I finished my picture of a fierce lion in Africa on the plains. When I was drawing it I felt like I was the lion being fierce." Glenn's time spent with a picture helps him experience the work and bring life to the fish in the picture: "I stare. There is talking around me but I continue to stare. There is a beautiful fish with perfect contrast in front of me. The coral around it makes me think of rainbows with all the variety of color there is. He quickly swims, darting from side to side."

Students return to favorite books and works of art—van Gogh's *Postman Roulin* and *Starry Night,* O'Keeffe's flowers—to copy, to imagine, to learn.

Sketching and Writing the Images

I focus on the images that a writer creates with words as I read books when we meet on the rug. I suggest that students close their eyes and look at the images the words create in their mind. I ask them to think about the words and how they might make a picture from the ideas. Students bring their sketch journals to the rug and sketch the images they see as I read. This provides a way to connect a writer's use of language to creating images and pictures.

Tyler sketches light, swirling circles as he listens to the words of *The Same Wind* by Bette Killion. He writes that this sketch leads him to a new kind of picture—a large, colorful abstract painting: "Today I made a picture of a bright moon and storm clouds about to cover it and a pond with flowers and cattails next to it." Courtney copies a line she likes as I read, then uses the words as part of the collage she creates propelled by the image and feeling she got from listening to the book. Rosie's painted bursts of color surround a copied passage. Students use images—in words and pictures—in their work, just as writers and artists do.

Students respond to literature by making a picture. David does a chalk pastel drawing of the cover of *James and the Giant Peach* by R. Dahl, his favorite book. Gwen uses her artist's notebook to plan out her response to a scene from the book *Gwinna* by B. Berger. Nick does a careful drawing of an episode from his favorite book, *Matilda* by R. Dahl, then writes, "I picked this book because of the good pictures even though it had no pictures. I saw them in the words." Responding visually to a book helps students see the images they read and understand the setting. They link the images they get as they read with the images they place on paper, then with the ones they write in words.

Starting Conversations

We read *A Blue Butterfly: A Story About Claude Monet* by B. Tord, and learn that Monet thinks nothing is impossible, that he observes things in a unique way, and practices his art constantly. We read *Camille and the Sunflowers* by L. Anholt, about Vincent van Gogh, and learn that he struggles because others do not appreciate his style of painting but that he keeps going. Books provide lessons and lines for my students and for me. We make connections between what we experience and what we believe.

A quote by Matisse is chalked onto the blackboard next to today's date. A passage from van Gogh is printed on a large poster in the gallery. Georgia O'-Keeffe's way of painting flowers so large that they seem to spill over the edges of the canvas is a minilesson to help fourth graders use drawing to observe the growth of plants over thirty days. Ursula then uses her scientific drawings as studies for a large painting of an iris. Mark writes that copying a painting by Winslow Homer makes him feel "daring," helps him go beyond what he thought he could do. An artist and his work, her work, become mentors to students as they work.

I make picture books part of the rehearsal for learning at the beginning of class and part of my learning and preparation for teaching. The work of authors and illustrators, the ideas and images of artists, provide a context and conversation for the work to follow. Art begins to inform and extend learning.

As a third grader works on a collage, I reach for *Frederick,* by Leo Lionni, and show her how her picture reminds me of Lionni's style. Artists help Deborah think about her own frustrations in trying to do her work: "I wonder how Picasso and Matisse put up with all of their mistakes? What happened when people like them didn't have an idea? What would they do? What if their minds were blocked with words, and pictures just weren't there?" Students integrate the language, the words, the thinking of artists into their own work.

Using Leads in Context

Art and literature model how to write description. Lines and ideas provide leads for writing. After listening to *The Magic Bicycle,* Rosie draws a close-up of a pair of boots in front of a sled and writes: "My sled lies still for the first time today. A shadow of trees stands silent as the wind catches its breath. The rough bark that I cling to holds hopes, memories, and fears. I tried to make my picture look fuzzy and distant so it would look like a memory."

Tyler's copy of a painting in the gallery immerses him in the painting and in his work: "I see water rushing up the beach's flat sand on a dark misty night. The moon peeks through the clouds and its beam shines down. The water sparkles in the moon's bright light. Branches from a tree show in the corner of my eye. The rocks stick out of the water and then they sink back down when the water spills over them."

Courtney's close-up of a flower in chalk pastel is a copy from a picture book, and her writing emerges from connections she makes with the ideas of Georgia O'Keeffe: "To see, to look really closely at a picture, takes time. At a glance you

"Courtney"

She worked on a collage today.
She had gone to the c-cart
and taken papers. Are both
of cut papers were "stuck"
together and she chose
to stick them on her
page. She had the book
Owl Moon open and I didn't
see the connection between
her collage and the book
I later rehearsed and saw
the image of a person smearing
as she continued to glue—
She was doing her interpretation
of the pages from Owl Moon
and the stick was part of the landscape

when it was time to clean up
Courtney still had
the book on her
table and I said
"you need to put
it away." "No—"
she replied.
"I need to record
something when
we write."
And so—
Courtney sat
back in her
classroom
with her
collage on
the table—
her journal
opened—
Owl Moon
on her lap
and she
copied a
line from
the
book
onto
her
collage.
Now
she
writes.

think what it is but if you take a journey, you'll explore things all of the time. You will see things you didn't even see before when somebody shares with you. You need enough nerve to share your ideas and extend them beyond others in drawing and writing."

An O'Keeffe reproduction on a postcard inspires Jane's work in swirling layers of tissue paper. She adds writing to the design of the swirls: "When I look at my picture I see things flying about my page. I see a tornado of thought. I see a blur of a rainbow. I see the dawn sky on my page. I see a fleet of living creatures. I see orange as lively as you and me. I see a bird's-eye view of a crowd. I see a field of wild flowers. I see spilled paint all over the page. I see a work of art."

The work of artists and writers inspires student work and gives me ideas for leading them into writing. Student thinking, imagining, writing, are different in the context of artists and writers.

Going to Museums

Learning at an art museum—for children, teachers, and parents—extends the learning that begins in school. Students prepare for the trip for the entire year as they learn about artists and art, learn to look and discuss what they see, learn to make their own art, practice drawing to see and writing to think and reflect, share their work, get responses, meet deadlines, and exhibit their work. Teachers prepare as they keep their own sketch journal and make the work of artists and writers part of what they learn and teach.

I give a workshop to prepare parents for the field trip, and it adds to the many ways they learn about the connection between art and learning throughout the year. At the museum a parent sees the artworks through her own eyes and through the eyes of the children in her group as they discuss the works they are attracted to, draw them, and write about them.

Classroom teachers and I collaborate as we prepare children for the trip. We show slides of works in the museum's permanent collection and give students time to respond orally or in writing. They practice thinking and talking about the works they will see. Before going to an exhibit of Georgia O'Keeffe's work, teachers share information about the artist and her work and ask students to do close observations of a flower. Drawing a simple machine to help figure out how it works prepares us for the Leonardo da Vinci exhibit.

We emphasize our expectations: write and sketch about several works as you move through the galleries in small groups, accompanied by a parent; do not touch works of art; talk in whispers or quiet voices; stay with the adult at all times. Informing everyone involved—parents, teachers, museum personnel— helps make the trip a successful and rich learning experience.

On our museum trips, there are no large groups of students being led by docents. There is silence, focus, and demonstration of purpose. Students, teachers, and parents select paintings or sculptures that interest them and sketch them or write about them.

Tyler and Tom sketch *Night Cafe* by Vincent van Gogh. Tyler writes in his sketch journal, "I can tell this is [van Gogh's] because in most of his pictures he puts streaks around the lights. This also reminds me of Degas. They both draw very moody pictures."

Katie takes possession of a Mondrian painting as she walks up to it, examines it closely, sits on the floor, and begins to write.

Ursula writes in her sketch journal, "I enter this picture . . ."

Teacher Peter von Euler captures O'Keeffe's *The Lawrence Tree,* while student Margaux and her mother sit next to each other on a bench and each sketch *Doorway to the Sea* by Edward Hopper.

Tyler and Tom share an interest in a painting by van Gogh because they did their own version of van Gogh's work in the classroom. Tyler is able to describe the feeling in the painting and connect the painting with the work of another artist. Katie's tool for observation is her writing. Ursula uses a skill that will empower her to go to museums on her own, seek out works of art that allow her to enter into a conversation with them, to find her own meaning. Margaux's sketch will lead her back to the artists workshop to do her own painting of the Edward Hopper scene, learning more about the techniques she saw being used there.

After a trip to the Yale University Gallery, Christine McGovern asks her second graders to use their notes and sketches to do a finished picture and develop a piece of writing about the picture. She connects the assignment with units on character development and the descriptive senses. Jennie's picture is *Yosemite Valley* by Albert Bierstadt: "I row through the river. The sun shines. My mouth starts to water. The wind is blowing in my face and I shiver. My whole body aches." *John Biglin in a Single Skull,* by Thomas Eakins, inspires Jason: "His face is dripping with sweat. . . . He is weak, but he has to row more. He sees the island and lets the boat glide up into the sand of the beach." Inspired by the work of the artists and familiar with the process of looking, responding, and imagining, these second graders did some of their best writing of the year.

After museum trips, parents are asked to fill out an informal questionnaire about images, conversations, and discoveries. One parent remembers: "My daughter and I did drawings of Winslow Homer's *The Red Feather* and we discovered, as we looked, that on the hillside covered with wildflowers where the woman wearing the cape and the hat with the red feather is standing there is a shaggy dog in the grass at her feet." Together, parents and students make

Margaret Young sketching "Doorway to the Sea"
Edward Hopper

discoveries, respond to the emotion in a painting, take ideas back to the workshop to continue their own learning in art and writing.

Understanding the Language

Marc's third-grade sketch journal has several pages of quotes from artists: a
thought from van Gogh about needing pictures to express himself, a tip from
Seurat about brush strokes, Cézanne's plan for his own art supplies. These ideas

help Marc when he is stuck. He writes, "The artist's writing may be hard to follow for a lot of people but not me. I knew exactly what each word and each sentence meant. . . . It made me think about how I felt making my own pieces of writing and drawings. I understand the artist's language."

I am puzzled, then, when he writes, "The moon may have water and many new possibilities" as the headline for the first page of his fourth-grade journal and continues, "Scientists think they have detected water on the moon. . . ." He explains that he has always wondered about the moon and things in outer space, and this news was recently reported in the newspaper. "Leonardo used his [notebook] to wonder. I thought it would be a good way to begin."

Marc and all students need mentors, whether they are in science or math, art or literature, sports or professions. The lessons they learn may be how to see, how to use paint, how to copy a likeness. But in the process, they make connections between copying and describing, looking and imagining, doing art and living life.

During the summer before she enters middle school, I receive a postcard from Gwen, an expert at collage. On the front of the card is the burst of *Red Poppy* by Georgia O'Keeffe. Gwen has written on the back:

Dear Ms. Ernst,

Yesterday I went to the Met. Unfortunately there weren't many collages, but the Klee drawings were great. He transferred the ink onto another piece of paper to make it look smudgier. Talk to you soon!

Love, Gwen

There are a lifetime of reasons for going to museums, and we find connections between drawing, wondering, science, and discovery. The language of artists, their ideas, and their ways are woven throughout our conversations, our writing, and our pictures. We not only learn to appreciate art, we connect with it, respond to it, describe it, see it, learn lessons from it, and use it in our writing.

Begin now to make artists and writers your mentors so they can be among the many teachers of your students. The lessons are many, spontaneous, and surprising.

Experience for Yourself

- ☐ Look through picture books to get ideas for pictures and writing.
- ☐ Read a picture book. Notice techniques of the illustrator. Always ask, *How can I get the same effect?*
- ☐ Read a book. Listen for the word images.
- ☐ Read a book to get an idea for a picture.

- Read a picture book to examine a technique.
- Respond to a book through pictures or writing.
- Copy a picture from a book to learn from the artist/illustrator.
- Close your eyes as you listen to a story or poem and watch the pictures in your imagination.
- Sketch while listening to a book being read.
- Collect postcards of art reproductions. Laminate them and keep them in a box to use as ideas for stories or pictures.
- Make a gallery of art reproductions in your home or classroom. Include poems and quotations by artists.
- Study an artist in depth.
- Select a work of art and look at it and think about what you see, what you feel, techniques you notice as you look.
- Use your imagination to "go inside" a work of art. Describe what you find there.
- Tell the story in a painting or work of art.
- Copy the work of an artist. Write about what you learned while copying it. Write about why you chose that particular painting.

9

Spaces for Learning and Teaching

I'm flying along galleries, stories come alive, pictures are lining the walls. My hands glide along, my mind wires with excitement as I fly, everywhere, every which way. I see something, either writing or pictures. All are my favorites, all are pretty, all are glowing with pride. They are mine.

—Rosie, age 9

A framed picture of a lion, done by second graders Alicia and Samantha, sits on the counter of the gallery. This lion is part of a tradition that began when Cary copied it from a book and other students admired it and began copying from Cary. Students copy from each other. They sprawl on the rug to copy pictures on the sharing board—a watercolor landscape by Natalie or a cat surrounded by a rainbow of colors by first grader Katherine. The work on the sharing board shows the range of what students can do and teaches lessons and techniques— filling in the whole page, washing a watercolor across the background, using perspective. Nick, a fourth grader, walks into the art room, and immediately recognizes Nellie's attempt to copy the *Mona Lisa* by Leonardo da Vinci. Nick and kindergartner Nellie have a common learning experience.

As a fourth-grade class returns from visiting the all-school exhibition, many students write about the imagination they notice in the pictures created by kindergartners and first graders. This observation becomes a lead for writing about imagination and the purpose of art. Frank writes, "I think when we start to get older we gain imagination and lose it. What I mean is we lose the thoughts about Big Bird and Santa. But we gain thoughts about country-sides and cities. I wonder what it would be like to get my old imagination back and think about more childish things."

During a
silent art workshop.

The dragon is
the teacher.

Natalie –
"I just got the
idea to
do a
collage
and when
Matthew
was talking
he said
"horse"
and I
decided to
do a farm.
Annie

Patrick and Jordan move back
and forth as they work on their
dragon. There is such
talking, pointing, movement

Laura – watercolor
"I've just started collaborating with Annie & Natalie.

When classrooms and schools establish structures and spaces (exhibitions, galleries, students sharing as guest artists in another class) whereby children can share their work, learn from one another, and begin to use what they learn to teach one another, children develop an appreciation for all artwork. Students learn to talk about their own work, share their process, and listen to one another. This builds the classroom and school community. Setting deadlines for these experiences propels work to new heights.

Note the many spaces for teaching and learning throughout our school. Listen and watch as children learn from one another and help build the learning community.

The Artist's Share

Before I can begin the minilesson, Courtney raises her hand and asks, "Can I share?" She stands next to me to explain, "My dad and I went for a hike in the woods behind our yard. We found a trail and saw a fox den. Today I am going to draw that fox den." Children—and adults—need to go public with their work, share it in a community where they feel comfortable, where they know they can share ideas, get a response, change as a result of that response, and show their process and product. Artist's share provides a structure in the artists workshop for students, and sometimes teachers, to go public when they need to.

In artist's share, held at the beginning of artists workshop, a student volunteers to share her work, finished or in progress, explain how she made the picture, where she got her idea, why she wants to share it, and ask for a response from the audience. Conversation is based on what children see and wonder. It gives the students and me insight into the picture and the person and teaches many skills—how to talk publicly, listen and respond, think about process. It nurtures apprenticeships in the classroom and provides a means to assess the child's progress.

I introduce artist's share by putting one of my own pictures on the easel at the edge of the rug and then sitting in a chair about ten feet from the easel—artists must get distance from their work to see it in a new way. I describe the work, ask for a few responses, and remind the students that telling me *I like your picture* does not really help me see or think about my work. "I need to know what I have done well, what you notice, what ideas you get as you look at my picture," I explain to them.

Throughout the year I continue to model appropriate and helpful kinds of comments by raising my hand to respond. I also go to the easel and teach technique directly—how a student paints in perspective or uses shadow or reflection in the picture.

As students begin to develop confidence in their classroom community, they place unfinished pictures on the easel, ask for advice, and point out their own mistakes and how they use them.

Anna, age eight, clearly shares her intention about her picture of a vase of flowers when she explains, "It was hard to get the shape of the vase. I used oil pastel and was careful not to blend in the colors. I made the water in the vase with colored pencils because I thought it looked better than pastels." She reads from her notebook: "Today I went back home to look at the tulips on my kitchen table," then calls on classmates for their response. "I like the way you put the pot on the table. I notice it is tipping over." Anna quickly points out, "It was hard to put the table in the picture and I didn't know I would do that, but the pot was in the air when I finished it." Artist's share shows how children solve problems.

When Lindsay asks if Anna really went home to see the flowers, Anna answers, "I didn't really go home. I could see the tulips in my mind." Anna's writing lets her imagine.

In another class, Lauren shares her connections to Jacob's picture of mountains. "It reminds me of my picture when I did artist's share. Mine was the water, though." Artist's share provides a way for children to learn to talk to one another and make connections, which is important in building community.

When I ask Margaux why she is so eager to do an artist's share, she answers that she wants to see what it is like. A structured opportunity for students to speak publicly is a challenge for some. It implies that sharing is important. It propels students like Margaux to try it, and gives others an opportunity to share their success.

R. J. says, "I think this is the best picture I have ever made. I got my idea from a picture in the gallery. I have never put air touching the ground before." A picture of a house with the entire background filled in, the sun in the middle of the sky, is an important marker in his progress and makes him need to share. Hearing responses—"I like the sun here instead of the corner" and "I like the way the sun shines down on the house, lighting up the red"—adds to R. J.'s sense of success. Progress, accomplishment, and observation take on new definitions.

Liz shares the range in her styles and the diversity in her portfolio as she places three pictures on the easel and asks her fourth-grade class, "What do you see?" Bold streaks of color in a kindergarten picture take on new meaning when Max shares that he got the idea for his picture "when my dad and I were boating. The sun was setting." Steven takes an intense interest in Paul's work, approaching the easel to get a better look.

Children share their ability to use language to describe, often poetically. Frank describes his collage: "This is a whale in the late afternoon, jumping in the sunset. I put details in that you can't see. A fin. A lightish part of the sea by

Matt sprawls in a tangle on the floor sketching from the exhibition.

the shore, and the silver part around the left side of the picture is a rock." Conversation about pictures is a rehearsal for writing.

Through artist's share I learn that student work builds from year to year and student to student. When Matthew shares his black-pen sketch of a fence and a field, he announces that he got his idea from a fourth grader's picture that was on the sharing board last year. Matthew's picture leads John to create his own version in paint, and when he shares he quickly gives credit to Matthew.

All-School Exhibitions

All-school exhibitions—held about four times a year—are an opportunity for students to select a work from their portfolio to place on hallway bulletin boards. They are important spaces for extending teaching and learning to the entire school community. The deadline for an upcoming exhibition teaches the importance of working toward a product and often propels better work. A student's writing about the piece—why he chose it, how she made it, what it is about, what the title signifies—enables the school community to see meaning.

In combination, the students' writing, their pictures, and my signs explaining the work in and process of the artists workshop reveal that pictures are an important part of a child's world of learning and expression. By teaching students to "read an exhibition," I teach them to observe, assess, gather ideas, learn, write about, sketch and verbalize what they notice.

When Mary Kate, a fourth grader, returns from her hour-long opportunity to sit in silence and read the exhibition, she writes,

> *Today I looked at other people's pictures and I was amazed at how good these pictures were. I didn't know what some pictures were but when I read what it was I realized it looked exactly like it was supposed to. When I was copying a picture made by a five-year-old, I was amazed at how the picture was better than I could do, but I know that I should not compare my pictures with [those of] other artists.*

Reading the exhibition propels the work when students return to the studio. We share ideas we gathered, talk about things we noticed, and share the sketches we made. Giuseppi returns to do his own version of a watercolor pumpkin he sees in the hallway. Cary does an oil pastel interpretation of a black-pen drawing by Malcolm. Noah's owl on a branch is copied over and over by first graders. Some students choose to work in the small gallery outside the door to the artists workshop, copying a picture.

Exhibitions are an important way to communicate what happens inside the art room. Our first exhbition goes up in late September, for back-to-school night. I write about the exhibition in the weekly PTA newsletter and send notices to all the teachers. Just as Mary Kate begins to notice and respect the uniqueness of younger children's work, parents begin to feel the spontaneity, range, simplicity, and imagination of children's work that grows out of their choices and meaning.

Classroom Galleries

Classroom galleries extend publishing—illustrations allow children to go public with the whole story. When Analisa, a first grader, begins her story with a chalk pastel depicting a lunar moth, then writes about the moth that she caught with her father, both the words and the picture are necessary when she publishes her story. When pictures are central to the writers workshop, galleries are an important part of publishing.

"Honoring the Original" is the name Darcy Hicks gives to a gallery she has set up in her third-grade classroom. In it children display the entire series of pictures that lead to their final work. Other teachers and students learn from this work, for Hicks's door is open to all.

Christine McGovern's second graders estabish a gallery in the hallway outside their classroom. It becomes a space for learning as they invite other classes to visit. Fourth graders stand in silence in the hallway, sketch journals in hand, and take notes on the exhibition, which is called "Language Is Power." They learn how second graders use the skills of revision—they add detail and description. Laura's words change from "I ran past a bunch of trees" to "I heard behind me the tripping of a gigantic monster."

Christine's writing, which is part of the exhibition, explains how students use a picture to begin their writing or to help them see what they are writing about. Students become docents, explaining the process of their work to visiting classes. Kristi Blob's gallery shows the step-by-step process that takes her first graders from an idea in their sketch journal to a finished picture and piece of writing. Classroom galleries provide ways for children and teachers to teach and learn from one another, peer to peer and across grade levels. Students expect to share their learning with others, and that expectation changes the school community.

Open Classrooms

Learning grows when individual students lead guest minilessons or when one class teaches another. When Lynn Gehr sees her second graders struggle with writing poetry, she asks Peter von Euler's fourth graders to come in and share how they move from a picture to a poem. Elizabeth brings with her three large cards, each containing a word that is signaled in her picture and that led to an idea in her poem—*sun, dog, tree*. Margaux explains that making a picture of a poem after she writes it helps her rethink the poem. Zoe explains that she moves back and forth from picture to poem as she composes. Chris outlines the seven steps he uses in going from picture to poem. Asking the fourth graders to teach clarifies what they know about their own process, and what they say changes what the second graders produce.

Respect for the work of others and rigor in writing emerges as children learn from one another. First grader Lauren gets writerly responses about her picture book about animals when she reads it to fourth graders: "There was lots of description in the beginning, but you need more details about the bobcats." "The pictures are good. I couldn't draw using anything but pencil in first grade." "You wrote down what the animals looked like but see if you can make the words more poemlike."

When first graders Cameron and Brian share their large rain-forest picture to a class of fourth graders, the conversation between the boys and the class shows everyone's knowledge. "The dark parts of the picture are the understory," Cameron and Brian explain. A fourth grader offers, "Your picture looks like it is not standing still."

Pointing out movement in a picture, sharing what one knows, telling an artist or writer what is working and what isn't, changes the way children think about learning, the way they publish, revise, and write. And these exchanges provide teachers with insight into what a child knows.

Children teach their parents. Darcy Hicks invites parents to an opening of her class's exhibition. Each child's space in the gallery has an envelope into which parents can place their written responses. Dawn Damiani asks parents to participate in an artists-and-writers workshop in which several children explain their process in connection with works displayed in the classroom gallery.

Assemblies

School assemblies provide a space for going public with the work from writers and artists workshops. Music teacher Sarah Guterman invites students to show pictures and writing from throughout the year in an end-of-year assembly. Slides of artwork flash on the screen on the stage—colorful geometric designs, chalk pastel fireflies, landscapes, sunsets, lizards, toucans, flowers—as children move to the microphone to read their words during breaks in the music.

A selection of lines from student writing about what art is and what imagination is delivers a message about the importance of art in learning. "Imagination is very hard to explain," Kathleen begins. Other students follow:

"If feels good when I draw because it brings back memories."

"To me imagination is when my brain thinks up something exotic and my common sense tells me it's crazy."

"In art you can make things happen. If you add something you totally change the picture. The same in writing."

"Art paints something in my mind so I can look back. Art is how you say things in different ways, how you turn chairs into mountains and you into yourself."

"I saw a thing on the bus. I saw the jetty, clouds in the sky, beams of light hitting the water. That's my next idea for a picture."

"Art is a time when you're not in the room but in your picture, discovering the world beyond."

"Art gives you the ability to make doors open with a brush stroke and have your wildest dreams come true with a dot of marker."

"I do not think I'm losing my imagination now that I'm in fourth grade. It shows in my pictures."

An assembly informs parents by demonstrating the link between art and learning. It is evidence of teacher collaboration, and even when it is held at the end of the year, it propels next year's work.

Public Spaces

Exhibitions outside the school are an additional opportunity to teach the importance of art in learning. They are an opportunity for people in the community to learn how to read an exhibition, discover firsthand the importance of showing process and product, and realize the power of children's forms of expression.

Fourth graders work hard to prepare for an exhibit at the nature center in July. The deadline pushes Billy to paint with intensity. "I wish we could have school until August," another student offers as preparations for the exhibition move beyond the end of the school year. Tyler slips me his journal to share the discovery he made in sketching the ruffed grouse, and Andrew struggles to make his drawing the best it can be because this exhibition is going beyond the hallway galleries to a more public space.

When exhibitions are held at the town hall (perhaps as part of a townwide art show) or at state legislative buildings, it is essential to include an explanation of the process, to show the audience why they may be looking at an unedited page from a sketch journal or at a series of pictures that lead to a piece of writing. It takes the children's pictures, along with their words and mine, to get the message across.

Stretching the Learning

Children expect to learn from one another and to teach what they know. That expectation changes the way they produce and prepare for their work tomorrow or next year. They expect to learn from pictures in the gallery, from those resting on the easel by the rug. Passages on posters in the art room, written by former fourth graders, inform students who work there now. Alicia's thoughts on revision still teach:

> *A picture helps me to revise because if I didn't have a picture it's like having no idea. If you have a piece of writing that doesn't have a picture, you can put in some capitals and periods, and maybe some spelling needs to be fixed. But to me that's not revising. Revising stretches a piece far out, and without a picture you can't do that.*

Lions, toucans, landscapes, and designs that flash on the screen in the auditorium at the end of the year find their way into the pictures of next year's students. The memory of a fourth grader who came to a second grader's class to share will push the second grader to want to do the same when he is in fourth grade. Children open their sketch journals for visitors to read and are eager to take time to share what they are doing.

Exhibitions, galleries, artist's share—all spaces structured for teaching and learning—stretch the learning in a school and community "far out," beyond the school and the limitations of the end of the school year or graduation.

Experience for Yourself

- Look closely at a painting in a museum or in your classroom gallery. Describe what you see—colors, shapes, stories, ideas. Now move back about ten feet and again describe what you see. What differences are there in the two descriptions?
- Place a picture you have made on an easel or a shelf and then step back about ten feet. Describe what you see. How does the picture change from when you were making it, working close to it?
- Ask a friend to share a picture she has made. As she describes the picture, how she made it, what it means, write down what she says. Write a reflection on what you learned about the person. (Sharing a picture is sharing information about yourself.)
- Share a picture. As you listen to others respond to your work, think about what comments are helpful to you. Write them down so you can model them for your students.
- Have each student select one work to exhibit. Ask them to title the piece and write a description of the picture, how they made it, and why they selected it. Keep track of the choices students make (this is an important part of their assessment).
- Copy passages from student journals that show their thinking and make these an integral part of an exhibition.
- Send a note home telling parents about an exhibition; invite them to an "opening."
- Visit an exhibition early some morning or late in the day, when no one else is around. Write down the stories that come to your mind. Think about your learning, the layers of meaning there.

10

The Challenge of Choice

A man that I met told me that he didn't discover that he was a good artist until he was out of college. His art teacher made him do things, so he never knew what he could do.

—Grant, age 9

Giving children choice in the classroom is a challenge. Children are more excited about and focused on work when it is theirs. Choice propels children to work on a project over time and recognize their own steps and strides in process and progress. Their choices raise questions for me about what I teach, create tensions about the product, and expose concerns about expectations. Choice drives my ideas for minilessons and my prompts for getting my students to write about their work. The solutions that I develop for dealing with choice come from the learning I gain as I ask children questions, talk with colleagues, or open the door to visitors. These solutions lead me to raise my expectations for what children can do and what I can teach. The challenge of choice constantly changes my classroom.

Children want choice. A student new to the school asks, "You mean I can make whatever I want?" He is excited but hardly knows where to begin. In many cases, whether he is six or seven or nine, it is the first time in his life he has ever gotten to choose what picture he will make at school. Choice is not part of his learning history. My job is to show him and all my students where to begin and to teach them  that choice is not freedom but responsibility. When I move to the edge of my chair and say, "I am concerned about the choices you are making" or "I am thinking about not giving choices today," my students pay attention.

Join Mrs. Williams, who is visiting from another school and wants to learn about the process of the artists workshop, how choice works and its value to children. Experience the tensions, questions, and solutions that arise for me as I answer her questions and deal with the challenges of choice.

Teachers Have Different Beliefs

Mrs. Williams's visit points up the differences between her beliefs and mine. She takes pride in the projects that she devises, the assignments she gives her students, and the pictures and products her students produce. Her beliefs drive the questions she asks: *How do kids value choice making? Where do they get ideas? How do you control product? What is the difference in the meaning of art for these kids and for mine? How do you teach technique, skills, art history?* She explains, "I give my students 'free choice' once they finish their project for me, but I am never satisfied with the results."

Making choices and coming up with ideas are skills that we must teach, not rewards we offer after the real work is finished. I believe that when choice is at the center of a workshop—artists or writers—children take responsibility for their work, invest more time and effort, and are willing to critique themselves, take criticism, revise, and work harder to improve. I know that the work of professional artists and writers grows from the choices they make, and I know that deadlines, high expectations, and peer response is fundamental.

I can never be sure of the work that students will do in a given class. It changes from week to week. A student who has experienced little success can suddenly make a breakthrough, while a heretofore hardworking student can come to the workshop with no idea and sit looking through the "library of ideas" for an entire hour. I can do a minilesson that no student picks up on. A student's idea revealed during an artist's share or an informal conversation can change what I know, do, and expect as a teacher. When I learn that a student needs quiet or wants to begin with writing, it changes what I expect of the entire class. I believe in staying in close, modeling, urging, praising, and remaining open to surprise.

Mrs. Williams's visit creates an added tension for me as I work. Will how I answer her, what I say, and what she sees confirm her own beliefs or change what she does in her classroom? During and after her visit, I challenge my own beliefs and renew my own questions about the learning that goes on in my classroom. The children and their answers help me understand more about choice.

Children Think Choice Is Important

Mrs. Williams explains to a fourth-grade class that she is curious about the difference between what her students experience and what these students experience here in the artists workshop. She asks them questions about choosing their own topic and material.

The fourth graders are reminded of their kindergarten experience, before they were introduced to choice in the artists workshop:

"She used to put out a basket and we had to draw it."

"It was boring when we had to do what the art teacher told us. I didn't look forward to art."

"I didn't really like it back then because we didn't get to see other people's work and ideas and say comments about them. In kindergarten the projects were exactly alike. There was nothing to say."

"Then, it wasn't being like a real artist. Now it is."

R. J. explains that in kindergarten he thought he knew what art was and was surprised when he had to do what the teacher did. He remembers only that he had to paste little mountains on a paper.

When Mrs. Williams asks my students what they do when they don't have an idea, they eagerly respond, "Look around the room, go to books, look at the paintings." Their answers are serious and thoughtful, and I hope that by asking our visitor to direct her questions to the students rather than to me helps her understand the shift in control—from a classroom centering on a teacher's projects and ideas to one centering on the students' expression of their own ideas. I want to believe that my students' understanding of art is authentic and complex and includes pictures they like and don't like, but I always wonder whether they are simply echoing what they hear me say.

From Belief to Practice

When the students go to work I notice a table of boys doing little more than talking loudly. Elsewhere, Ben holds a paintbrush in each hand, swirling colors across the page; he answers, "Nothing," when I ask him what he is thinking. Elizabeth paints little pictures around each letter of her name. Andrew makes a clay catapult. Someone purposely screeches his sneaker across the floor. Even though Grant continues his careful copy of an art card and Billy finishes his bold painting of a version of van Gogh's *Starry Night,* I am annoyed by the guises choice takes on this particular day.

I accompany the class back to their classroom and share my disappointment. "I am shocked by your work today. First you explain that you know the value of choice but then you show little responsibiltiy in making choices." My comments are the impetus for leads for writing: *What is art for? Capture a moment from today's art class, bring that moment back, and then write about how you can improve.* I reluctantly offer "your choice" as the final lead.

As we write in silence for twenty minutes I wonder what Mrs. Williams is thinking. If the teacher assigns a project, is she satisfied that learning has occurred when the project has been satisfactorily completed? Do students really care about the work that results? What did this fourth-grade class learn?

For my students, art doesn't end when they finish the project or when they leave the art room. Writing after art class pushes them to continue to learn as they rethink their time in art. They see from my concern that I am interested in their thinking, not just their product.

Winston writes a description to go with his picture that ends, "My head rests down on a thousand blades of grass. I fall asleep." Claire describes the challenge of choice this way: "If you don't have an idea then it is hard not to interfere with others." Vicki writes to prepare for her next art class. Dan's confession that he fools around because it is too loud in the art room prompts me to consider assigning seats and establishing new noise-level expectations. Grant reveals that he has been working on the same picture for over a month and that he is "having a big breakthrough in art, probably one of the biggest. I am learning patience, doing one thing at a time."

Writing helps us all reflect and prepare for the next art class. It underlines the responsibility for students and teachers and is part of the learning experience. But my questions and my students' answers are not a prescription for Mrs. Williams. She must ask her own questions and get her answers from her own students.

Structuring Choice

Children teach me lessons about choice. I ask students to write about how choice helps and how it doesn't help. They want choice. It lets them find their own area of interest and be comfortable with learning. But limits are important, too. One student writes, "Choice is a good thing but it is not letting me go very far, I need to know how to do some of the steps in sketching, it is not helping me learn how to get better at some of the things I like, I think there should be a limit of what we can do and cannot do."

Mike writes, "Having choice is different. Drawing monsters works for me!" Choice provides a way for a student to begin working in an area of comfort. However, lest he get stuck in that comfortable place and not move beyond it, I must frame choice with repeated minilessons on technique, set limits at times, and establish structures to push the product. I need to urge my students to go beyond where they are comfortable.

The only sound is the flipping of books - sketching - reading - looking. Miss Ernst. Do we have to read or can we just look?
Kathleen sketches front of Trapiss. Many write.
"I like the way.

when we met on the rug — they sat with their sketchbooks. Some were sprawled over the tables. Lauren copied the passage in box on blackboard. I asked them how their journal journey was going

Understanding the Goal

Know a child's intention

I am concerned when Janet, an accomplished painter, chooses a partially drawn tulip for the end-of-year exhibition. Her writing explains her reason: "I've never drawn a good plant from nature, but now I have. Even though I think my lion picture is best, I don't have a feeling that I've completed a task." And Gwen, after many months of becoming an expert at collage, chooses an abstract painting for the exhibition. She writes that she wants her audience to look closely at her work and wonder how she made it. She hopes to inspire others. Students' sense of audience gives them a purpose; a sense of accomplishment can be more important to them than displaying their "best" work.

Ask the right questions

First grader Matthew asks to do an artist's share but has no idea which of his pictures will be the subject. I am surprised when he finally decides on a picture of two houses outlined in marker, but I understand when he tells me and the class that it is the first time he knew he "could fit two houses on one page." His first-grade classmates nod in agreement, and I learn the real skills important to children.

Learn the why *behind repetition*

During all of third grade Lee makes pencil drawings of monsters and sports figures. My endless attempts to get him to select something else fail. In fourth grade he changes to painting. "Why the change?" I ask him. He tells me that third grade, when he was new to the school, was the first time he was able to choose what he would work on and his goal was to have a thick portfolio. Now in fourth grade he sees his friends painting and wants to try it. He cautions me that it would not have been the same if I had forced him to paint. Peer influence is an important agent for change.

Encouraging Diversity

Children value a range in their work. Chris creates a carefully crafted collage—a pumpkin drawn in strong line, torn-paper leaves on a squiggly vine—and the next week returns to pencil drawings of airplanes dropping bombs. The pride he has in his work helps him ignore my alarm and displeasure when I question him about the change from one week to the next. "I know I can really make anything I want once I put my mind to it," he tells me. He explains that he likes to do things totally different, even change from a peaceful picture to a violent one. This "helps me clear things out in my mind," he offers. My students' explanations help me see the value of pictures I may not "like," and my questions help my students understand that I expect them to think about what they are doing.

A classroom with choice must make room for both teacher expectation and student interest. When students are interested in and excited about their own work, they make discoveries and carry out ideas that go beyond a teacher's assignments. Glenn writes, "I love variety in art. I don't care what the variety is, I just love variety. For example, my pointillism window picture. Who would have thought up a pointillism window picture? This year I want to discover some kind of new technique. I wonder if I ever will?"

Urging Experimentation

I introduce clay for the first time in a minilesson, demonstrate how to use it, and urge students to experiment—turn and push the clay to get ideas—and not be concerned about making something the first time. My focus is on how the students and I will handle clay as a new choice.

At the end of class, Matthew is eager to share what he has written: "Today I tried oil pastels for the first time. I didn't like how it came out." I discover that he applied my comments about clay to his fear of using oil pastel. He took a risk and attempted a lion picture like Cary's, one he had admired for weeks. When I share Matthew's story with other classes, they immediately relate to the fear and excitement he felt and are sure he will try oil pastel again. The lessons learned by individual students push others to try new things and experiment.

Placing Limits

Sometimes it's okay to limit the options. Peter only draws monsters. He writes about these huge, graphic "things" with bulging eyeballs and long, pointed fingers or hands. He knows his class anticipates his next goulish tale. My many attempts to get him to return to the exquisite wild birds and animals that he previously drew fail. When his mother reviews his portfolio and imposes a two-month moratorium on monster drawings, Peter produces chalk pastel lions with brilliant purple backgrounds, paintings of flowers.

"Peter made a bouquet of flowers today! And did you see his lion?" Peter's classmates greet me one day as I enter their classroom. Children support, anticipate, even recognize individual style in a classroom in which choice and sharing is ongoing. They can support their classmates' monsters—repetition, predictability—but also the strides in their learning. The breakthroughs of one student are an accomplishment for all.

Students can be asked to stick with the same choice—a material, a topic, a genre—in order to develop expertise. When students enter the artists workshop

Andrew
Long

~~Dillon~~ Dylan Curtis

} I am purposely ending this journal with
a challenge for me as a teacher. This class comes
into the room each week, meets me on the rug,
and the entire meeting sets me up for tension.
"Is it almost done? Are you going to read
the whole story? Do we have to . Use oil pastel?
Why can't we use clay today? There is no focus —
or should I say the make-up of this class is such
that the kids are sort of meek — no real
trouble-causers, but there is no community .

and ask, "What is the new choice today?," I suspect that choice only means a potpourri of options with no real inquiry into what a material can do.

I require third and fourth graders to select a material and stick with it for one month. "Choose something you do not often use, something that you feel is a stretch." I give them one week to experiment, contemplate their choice, and think about why they will select it. I model the assignment by using colored pencils instead of my black pen for a month. "Color changes what I see, it slows me down. I feel self-conscious, off balance, and want to return to the freedom of my pen," I tell a class of fourth graders. I ask them to think about the challenges, their process over the month, and how they deal with the difficulties. Staying with the same thing teaches discipline and leads to understanding.

Kristen chooses to work with black pen for the month. She writes, "If you are free with your pen, you feel relaxed and concentrate on what you see, not on how you want it to look. I was able to think better with my pen flying and my mind followed."

At the end of the month students exhibit one piece from their inquiry and share the things they've learned:

> "The challenge was trying to be comfortable with the material and learn how to like it."
>
> "Smudging is a big problem with oil pastels."
>
> "You need to be patient and take your time."

Students begin learning to look at the details in using a material, give tips to others on what they are learning, and begin to understand what it means to deal with the problems they encounter as they work in a subject or material over time. Placing limits expands the knowledge of all.

Asking Questions, Waiting for Answers

Teachers need to stay open to surprise. Emma teaches me to be patient while students learn the meaning of choice and its responsibilities. She goes to work with clear focus on a picture that confuses me—half of the page is neat, brightly painted squares, the other half a design of lines, splotches of color, and a tangle of scribbled crayon marks. I have just presented a minilesson on drawing in contour—how to observe through drawing—and I wonder what is going on in her mind in the quiet classroom. I question my minilesson—why do so few students seem to pick up on the skills? how will they learn these skills? I wonder whether they really come with ideas, whether they are thinking. I question choice—does it lack structure? is there too much freedom?

The writing the students do, the planning and description that emerges from the pictures and the quiet, reveals the variety of learning styles in the classroom: "a picture of a sun that made me feel a little deep," "a picture of a plant titled *Green Life,*" "next art period I am going to draw a picture of the moon and a cliff with a wolf howling on it," "I copied a tree by Matisse," "I want to write a poem about my picture."

Emma's writing surprises me the most. Her picture shows the difference between this art class, which allows choice, and one in which projects are assigned. She writes about her former art class, "Every day it was the same. Today we will paint, today we will sketch, today we will do crayons. It got extremely boring." The side of her picture with neat colorful squares is titled "Boring," while the one with scribbled lines and blobs of color is labeled "Perfect."

We need to give students time to learn the lessons and the responsibilities of choice; they need to be allowed to write about the thinking behind their choices.

The Lessons of Choice

Mrs Williams confesses, "I could not teach in such an unstructured way." But it is not lack of structure that she sees. I teach choice—its lessons and responsibilities—I learn from the children, and I constantly create structures by which to resolve the tensions and challenges I observe and experience.

Here are some things you can do to ensure that choice doesn't become a free-for-all:

- Provide structures for sharing so that students can learn from one another and see the range and diversity of work.
- Make your expectations clear but stay open to the reason a child makes a picture you don't understand.
- Share your questions and frustrations with your class so they will understand the value you place on their answers and on improving your classroom workshop.
- Encourage students to try new things, but also ask them to limit their options, stick with one thing over time to learn the possibilities that grow out of discipline.
- Be patient and open to surprise, and *ask questions.*
- Teach conventions and possibilities, and model your own work as a learner.
- Let the tensions of choice keep your classsroom alive, a place where teaching and learning stem from inquiry and experience.

The choices children make today build on the choices they have made in the past. The learning history of your classroom will change as the work of today

When I took my
portfolio home –
to share –
my Mom said
"nice dinosaur"
but it is a
gorilla."

Best picture in portfolio

to make.
These 2 cats are
playing patty cake
This picture I don't
like but I usually
use crayons & not
paint

David

Kimmy Nicole
A picture from what we
saw
when we made this
together we got each
other to use
new things

Giancarlo.
Bird-O-Frankenstein

shooting star
These lines show
going fast.
I remember
my boat period
in K.

Vivian
A rose I made
to give to my
Mom

Max K.

Katie
I usually like to draw
mountains. At first I
made a hat
when Mrs. McGrail came
she said she goes to a
place that looks just like when Elif was in Pakistan teacher told her what?
this.

Talia – "I don't think it would be good
because you couldn't go into
your imagination."

Elif

Courtney
I love
that
flowers.

Anna
I made at beginning
of year. Same as
I made last
year. Last year
letter. I like the
checks but not

builds on the lessons learned from individual children, lessons that teach you why to impose limits and how to raise expectations.

Experience for Yourself

- Give yourself the choice of making a picture of anything you choose. Write to find the idea, to examine how you feel about making the choice. What are your fears? What helps you make the choice?
- Give yourself the option of selecting a material: paint, pencil, markers, crayons. Which do you choose? Why?
- Which art material are you reluctant or even scared to use? Why? Write about the feelings.
- Choose to work with a material that you fear. Experiment with it. Write about what you learn once you take the risk.
- Select a material and use it for one month. Each time you use the material, write about what you notice about the material, your process, yourself. Keep a record of your progress and at the end of the month look at how you have changed.
- Ask children why choice is important. Ask them to make a choice and write about why they chose it.
- Develop a monthlong unit in which you give your children choice, ask them questions about the process, and learn and change along with them.

11

Taking a Step Back

In first grade I just didn't think of taking my time. When I made a mistake I said, I have to start all over again. Now in second grade, I can make my mistakes into something.

—Cindy, age 7

My students step back when they write in their journal, ask a friend to hold up their picture so they can see it from a distance, or do an artist's share. They take a step back when they review their portfolios with their parents or prepare for an end-of-the-year artist's share. Any time we ask students to reread, relook, re-think work, we are asking them to assess what they do and show us what they notice. In return, we receive new understanding about what they are learning, what we are teaching, and how we can make the classsroom community better. These forms of assessment are opportunities for children, parents, and teachers to learn about progress and plan for the future.

Teachers also need to take a step back. We need to read back over our sketch journals to see how ideas begin, change, and take on a life in the classroom. We need to reflect on the notes we take about our classrooms and our students and use those notes to help us write narratives of progress that are much more complete than a report card. We need to meet with colleagues, ask them questions, listen to their questions, and let these questions raise new questions.

Stepping back benefits us and the children we teach. It helps us focus on the learning process and on an individual's learning history. We see the development of ideas, turning points, peaks, and strides in learning. Stepping back in the classroom and in the school community helps us value the process. It is another opportunity for learning and teaching; it brings about change.

Move in close and observe how I structure opportunities for my students and me to take a step back. As you do, think about similar structures you can develop to help you and your students.

Portfolio and Sketch Journal Review

Students take their portfolios home twice a year. In a minilesson students learn the review process and my expectations for it. I place a notice in the PTA newsletter that it is time for portfolio and sketch journal review to alert parents and to urge them to give the review their immediate attention.

The cover letter I prepare to accompany the portfolio/sketch journal is essential (see Figure 11–1). It gives the parents instructions, shows them what I expect and why, and provides information (again) about the artists workshop.

Looking for answers

Being really interested in the answer is the key to asking the question—in the portfolio review or in the classroom. Responses from reviews have helped me understand that students get most of their ideas from other students, that there is pride in knowing how to turn a mistake into something else, that most pictures have meaning, that there is great excitement in seeing that you know how to make something challenging, and that together the portfolio and sketch journal hold the story of progress. (The questions that accompany the portfolio/sketch journal change from year to year as I find that some answers are predictable and/or new questions arise.)

The mother of first grader Kate records Kate's response to the questions *How have you changed or grown as an artist since September? Which picture shows that? What has helped you get better?* "I have tried to be my best. In September I wasn't as good an artist as I thought I was. Then I kept trying and I got it. If I see a picture, I don't want to copy it all the way because I want it to be mine." Kate's response prompts me to think more about the issue of copying and teaches me that it is a way to begin, that students eventually move beyond just copying.

The clarity of a student's voice comes through in the reviews. When Kate is asked, "Is there anything else you would like to say?" she responds, "Yeah, it's like so amazing, because I see a picture and I want to draw it but I think I can't. But I really try hard and add some things in and I really take my time. If I don't like it I still keep on going. I try to fit everything in because I want it to be beautiful."

Extending learning

I talk with students about the review when they return their portfolios to the workshop. These conversations extend the assessment, tell me more, and em-

Dear Parent,

It is time for an artists workshop portfolio review. This is your child's portfolio, which he/she has kept since September. Please "review" the work with your child by looking through it with him/her and asking the questions listed below. This will give you a chance to see the work and talk with your child about it and will give me more information about him/her. I will also share these responses with your child's regular classroom teacher. The general information about the artists workshop presented below may help you with your review.

In the artists workshop, students may choose to express their own ideas using a variety of materials. We begin art with minilessons on how to use materials—paint, oil pastels, crayons, markers, clay—and share ideas by reading, looking at the work of artists, and listening to one another. Each student keeps a portfolio of all work—successes, experiments, challenges, even pictures that didn't work! (Clay projects are sketched and discussed in writing—the originals are taken home after they have been completed.)

With kindergartners, I focus on talking about the pictures to emphasize meaning. First through fourth graders write about their work in art in artist's notebooks and sketch journals. In many cases the writing extends into their regular classroom as well. (You may also want to ask your child whether you may look at his/her notebook/sketch journal.)

Reviewing your child's portfolio will give you a more complete picture of his/her work. Use the questions here as a guide to your conversation with your child, and write his/her responses in the space provided. Please return the question sheet and portfolio in two days. Thank you.

1. Tell me about some of the pictures in your portfolio. What are they about? How did you make them?

2. Which pictures and pages do you like best? Why?

3. Where do you get your ideas for your work?

4. Is there a picture that represents a challenge or shows how you have become a better artist, writer, or thinker?

5. How do you use your artist's notebook or sketch journal? What page are you proud of and why?

6. Is there anything else about your work that you would like to say?

FIGURE 11–1 *Cover letter for portfolio/sketch journal review*

phasize to the children that the review is important. Joseph offers, "My little brother brought his home. Boy, was there an improvement from the first of the year to his latest picture! The later ones had so much more detail. It just shows when you work hard you can really accomplish something." Reviewing work at home teaches parents and siblings about how pictures show meaning, how portfolios show progress over time; it increases respect for the uniqueness of individual work.

The portfolio review provides students with an audience and allows them to learn more about their own work by talking about it. Billy learns that his work can illicit feelings. "My mom thought my black-and-white picture was scary." Grant, used to getting responses to his work, shares his ability to listen to ideas: "I told [my mom] about each picture. Some of the pictures she gave ideas on, like to cut off the part where I spilled the paint on the alligator."

Children learn that their idea of art is different from their parents'. Winston says, "I showed my dad my portfolio first. He asked lots of questions. I was disappointed because my dad only seems to think professional artists do good work. I had some pictures that I really liked and he would just say they were okay. My mom really liked them." Winston's portfolio is evidence of his hard work—discovering things and solving problems. He knows that the thinking and meaning behind the picture is very important. I learn that I still have work to do in educating parents in the community.

Teaching parents continues as portfolios go home at the end of the year. I enclose another letter (see Figure 11–2) telling them about the final artist's share (see next section), inviting them once again to review the portfolio with their child, and suggesting that they conduct an artist's share at home. When children talk about their progress over a year, show the pictures that represent their journey of learning, they are looking at their own history and thereby establishing a foundation for the future.

Final Artist's Share

The last class of the year is a final artist's share. Each student selects a work— or several—that shows their progress as an artist, writer, and thinker over the year. For one hour (or longer if it continues in their regular classroom) children listen to and look at the progress of each of their classmates. Since there is no time for on-the-spot responses, students and teachers sit with their sketch journals open, ready to take notes, sketch the pictures that are placed on the easel, and write comments to share later.

When this final activity is part of the regular classroom as well, some teachers invite parents or a buddy class to be part of the audience. Preparing for the final artist's share, writing about the pieces selected, gives students a chance to

Dear Parents,

Here is your child's portfolio from the artists workshop. We had an exciting and productive year. "Artist's share" is an important part of the workshop. Students volunteer to place a work on the easel and talk about the work with the class. They then receive feedback from their classmates. It is an exciting opportunity for students to see work in progress, to learn from one another, and to use their skills in speaking to a group. Most important, it allows me to learn what children are thinking about their work.

We ended the year with a final artist's share in which each child shared at least one work from the year. In order to prepare, the children reviewed their portfolio looking for a successful picture or a picture they learned from or one in which they tried something new or one in which they made a discovery or one that surprised them. I asked them to think about where they get ideas for their work, what materials they most frequently use, and how their work has changed during the year. I suggested that they set a goal for themselves for next year and then select the picture or pictures they wanted share.

I'd like to ask you to review the portfolio with your child and use the above suggestions to frame your conversation. You, too, will then learn about your child's journey as an artist, writer, and thinker this past year.

FIGURE 11–2 *Letter to parents accompanying the end-of-year portfolio*

take a step back and review the work of the year and clues the classroom teacher, the parents, and me in on how the children themselves see their progress.

Learning their lessons

Final artist's share in Peter von Euler's fourth grade is a review of the students' work in artists and writers workshop. It is a collaboration between Peter and me and occurs in his classroom. To help the students prepare for the artist's share, I first ask them to quick-write on the topic, *What do you want others to understand about you and your work as you do artist's share?* Then we begin.

Jonathan confidently displays a watercolor of an iris, one of many flowers he has painted during the year; I learn the importance of being a recognized expert in a material and a topic. We empathize with Deborah's feeling of freedom as she shows a collage and describes her willingness to revise a section four times; her process of revision is as much a demonstration of her progress as her picture is. Lauren shares three pictures, each a "first": working with a partner, doing a collage, and experimenting with a material. Lauren teaches us that trying something new can be a giant stride that lets you really learn.

Tyler's drawing in "Ms. Ernst's style" shows how important it is for teachers to model techniques and their own learning. Caitlyn describes a day when she had no idea and I kept pushing her until she walked around the room to get ideas from her classmates. She tried to make a dog but it turned into a lion, a picture that "reminded me of that day." Success comes in the form of surprises and in subtle ways. Our job is always to provide the class with high expectations. Pictures hold memories of these moments of learning.

Glenn explains that his several pictures show two things, change and variety. When students look back they learn to analyze and categorize their own learning.

"The difference makes me proud"

John holds up his sketch journal, open to a page with a drawing of a branch. "I don't really like it," he begins, "but it stands out. I notice there is not much detail." Then he holds up a second picture done later in the year. "This one has more detail. I added shadows, and on this one I took my time." In order to show progress, a successful ending, we must show where we began. John knows that a picture does not have to be good to hold an important place in his learning history. A classroom community in which students are willing to risk showing where they started is essential.

Ursula places two pictures on the easel. One is a tree with a skinny trunk topped with blobs of paint in the colors of autumn. The tree is squeezed to the left of the page; the remaining space is white, empty. The other picture is large, a kitchen counter, vegetables, and a lobster; there is no white space, just color from edge to edge. Ursula reads from her quick-write: "I have found through the year that I have improved a lot. From the first picture and the last picture, there is a big difference. One has more thought and feeling, but the other feels quick and empty. These pictures both show the growth in me as an artist and thinker." Ursula needs to show both color and white space, empty and full, to give us the whole picture of her progress.

Maggie shows four pictures, telling us that she did not pick them because she is proud of them but because they show how she has changed: her beginning attempts, her frustration, how she remained calm and kept going. She also shows one that she worked on with a friend. She reads from her journal: "It is the difference that makes me proud. In this share I want to show difference, teamwork, spirit, and the ability of trying again. Struggle has brought me beauty, and effortless trying has brought me mistakes. But through experimentation and creative thoughts of my own, I have proudly finished my art year."

In the final days of the school year, when Peter and I feel we have taught everything we can, artist's share is a way to let our students be the teachers. These fourth graders prove to us how clearly they understand that their learning and progress is about more than making beautiful pictures. It involves courage,

Andrew did very well. I can see that Ander tried realy hard.

Jacquline tried very hard on it. I think its Great!

I like bens picture of the lion. I hope hes proud of his picture.

I like how Samantha was brave and to show us a picture that she thoght was a mistake

Sean and John did great! they gave us a good resan how they got there Idea.

magie did a great job of her picture. I'm proud of her!

Ursula did very well. She looks like she will probaly be a artist when she grows up.

---

struggle, risks, choices, mistakes, discoveries, and working as a community. It is the difference between "feeling empty," as Ursula said, and producing work with intention and meaning. Listening to them helps us step back and see their progress, what we teach them, what is important.

Students take notes and sketch pictures as they observe and listen to these final artist's shares. Their pages fill up with new ideas for pictures, comments to pass on to a friend, important lessons they have learned from their classmates. Lindsay writes, "I think that when I sketched everyone's drawings and wrote comments to them in my journal, it helped me see inside the pictures and notice new things about them. I also noticed that everyone in the class did different styles of painting, writing, and drawing."

I take a step back as I read the pages in my sketch journals to see my thinking, to understand the connections between what I am doing now and what I wondered weeks before. It is the way I review my teaching history. I reexamine my expectations for my own classroom as I meet with colleagues, listen to their questions about the connections between art and writing, and consider what I can do next to establish new structures, higher expectations. Stepping back helps me see the beginnings of ideas, rethink what I am teaching, change what I do, move forward.

David, a third grader, sits next to me as I read back over one of my sketch journals from the year before. "Look," I point to my quick line drawings and written notes from his final artist's share at the end of second grade. The jottings remind me of his presentation in front of parents; his classroom teacher, Lynn Gehr; his classmates; and me. He chose four pictures to show the "beginning, middle, and end of my work over the year." We look at the sketch of his picture "Bob's Steer Head."

"That was my best work in second grade," he explains. I have it hanging in my bedroom. Sometimes I read it and say to my mom, 'How could I be that good in second grade?' She tells me, 'You just were!' "

"Bob's Steer Head" came to be as a result of our visit to the Yale University Gallery and his interest in the work of Georgia O'Keeffe. Now in third grade, he is becoming an expert in pencil studies of things he observes. He frequently brings his writing from his classroom writers workshop to the art room. "Bob's Steer Head," his current artwork, his writing, and his knowledge of artists connect his learning history. "Bob's Steer Head" is a significant part of the foundation to his work. The notes in my own journal provide a similar foundation. They remind me that progress is slow and my current practice is a result of my earlier questions and obervations.

Other notes in my journal remind me of Paulina's two pictures—one of dancers with a bright yellow background, the other of a huge flower—and of when she approached the easel and read, "I think everyone is an artist. From the beginning of the year I made great pictures but in the middle of the year I started to change. I learned how to make my pictures come alive. Whenever we came back to the room for our writing after art I wouldn't worry about my writing. I'd go inside of it and describe what I saw." A seven-year-old has redefined art.

I remember Will showing his picture and saying that his good friend Charlie pushed him as an artist, convinced him to keep going when he was about to give up on his picture. Children acknowledge that friends are part of their learning history. I remember how Matthew, an expert at making animals, chose to show a landscape because he thought that both the picture and writing showed his progress. His "the sky tells its secrets to the mountains" is poetry.

Looking back at these pages helps me establish a continuum, a picture of the learning of Paulina, Will, Charlie, all my students. I am able to link the past to the future, assess my work as a teacher and the work of my students, see how important it is for children to develop a style, have a best picture, connect writing and art, and acknowledge the help of a friend. These ideas help me when I run into challenges in the classroom. They confirm what I believe and allow me to build on that.

Moving Forward

Reading back over my journal, meeting with teachers to reflect on our practice, hanging a picture on the wall, are ways to take a step back. The purpose is not to bring back what was but to help us rethink what can be. Unless we do this, our classrooms can become home to the routines of an empty process. Just as David's "Bob's Steer Head" reminds him how good he was in second grade, it also reminds him to continue to improve, to work toward a new picture that will mark his progress in third grade.

We teachers step back from our own practice when we meet to reflect on what we are doing and rethink what we can do. Kristi Blob helps move her first graders beyond writing "Today I made a picture of . . ." by rereading what she did the year before and listening to the minilessons others teachers use to push writing. Darcy Hicks develops new ways to teach revision. Peter von Euler finds that writing that was acceptable several years before is not a high enough standard today. Lynn Gehr admits her feeling of disconnection; she rarely comes to the art room, feels an emptiness in the routine of returning to the classroom to write. In the first years of the pilot project, the process was new and exciting; now she must move beyond that. As we learn to connect art and writing, the art room and the classroom, we establish new routines. But over time an empty routine is dangerous to growth. As classrooms change, as they include more art and more writing, I know I need to change my expectations in the art room. This process keeps our classrooms ever changing. It makes teaching an experience— a work of art in a way—that feels exciting and alive.

Experience for Yourself

    □ Make a picture. Write about what you see in it as you are very close to it. Then place it about ten feet away and write about what you see from a distance. Write about the ideas you get about changing the work.

- Make a list of the moments in your teaching history that are the hallmarks of your learning and work.
- Make a list of the expectations you have for your students in art or writing. How are they different from last year's expectations?
- How do you ask your students to step back?
- Ask your students to write about the piece of writing, the picture, or the book they believe represents their progress as a learner so far this year.
- Ask your students to select two pieces of art or writing that shows their growth as a writer, artist, learner.
- Meet with colleagues and write about the expectations you have for your classroom. Share what you have written with one another and then rethink your expectations in the context of what you learn from your colleagues.

12

Paying Close Attention

I really looked closely for details, almost seeing in a different way. It was almost like fishing and I reeled in a new way to draw and see. I got to have a new experience.

—Tyler, age 9

Each time I walk into my classroom I am a little bit off balance, prepared to pay close attention, keep my beliefs as my foundation, let my curiosity and desire to learn guide me through the day. I have no prescriptions for how to do this, only brief stories to show how paying close attention to children as they work—celebrating a success, challenging their lack of thinking, raising my expectations—helps me rethink what I do.

Rosie feels strongly that a change in her writing is as important as a change in her art: "In writing I've grown too. I write what my mind thinks and what I feel. I have changed from writing 'Today I made a picture of . . .'"

Justin knows that the collection of his writing and pictures shows his progress and learning history. He writes, "I draw a lot of birds and one picture leads to another. It has been like a chain. I used chalk pastel with paint in one so it would have the feeling of the sun coming through the clouds."

Courtney knows that she has grown from writing about pictures to picturing things in her writing. When she does her final artist's share she makes her audience anticipate her pictures—placing nothing on the easel, she says, "I observe more now. In second grade I wanted people to tell me what to draw. It helped me to look for ideas on my own. Sometimes Ms. Ernst would just lead me to the books and leave me there." She then reads a piece of writing and looks at her audience. "Does that writing give you a clear picture in your head? Now I'll show you the picture." How does she know to take the stride from writing about pictures to picturing things in her writing? How do I have the nerve to leave Courtney at the bookshelves looking for an idea, sometimes for the entire art class, and know that she will learn from that?

Reread the notes in your own journal as you think about what I think makes this possible. It happens over time and by paying close attention. It comes from an intense belief in community and a need to strengthen that community every day I teach. It comes from a belief in choice   a belief I question and research in my own classroom—and an understanding that to make choice work I must move in close and teach directly, then step back and watch carefully as my students learn the responsibilities choice brings. It comes from an authentic need to collaborate with teachers, inviting them into my classroom and going into their classrooms to learn. It involves learning from students—letting them know that I constantly have questions that they must help me answer.

Being Present

We need to be present in our own life in order to keep learning alive in our classroom. After a weeklong vacation, my sketch journal is my minilesson as I turn the pages and explain that I collect ideas when I go on vacation. I show the tiles surrounding the doorway of a store in a Portuguese town, the iron grillwork around the windows of one of the homes there, or the brilliantly intense poppies that grow wild in the fields along the roadside. "I wonder what ideas you collected while you were away from school," I muse.

When the class goes to work, Justin interrupts my thoughts with "It is hard to do hills!" As he begins to explain himself, I grab a piece of paper from the collage cart so I can record what he says. "I was at my relatives' house. Here's the hill, then there is a pond and down the hill is the house. At night when the moonlight bounced off the pond into the window, it seemed like a mirror. I'm focusing on the hill in my picture." His words reflect his poetic observation.

Michael listens to Justin, watches me take it all down on the scrap of paper, and offers, "I need a title for my picture."

"Tell me more and I'll help with a title," I say.

"When I was at my grandfather's I was running through the woods and the branches were slapping against my face. I decided to draw those branches." We agree on the title "Slapping Branches."

I turn the lights off to get everyone's attention. "How many of you are doing pictures of memories of your vacation?" Seven or eight students raise their hands, and I tell the class about Justin and Michael, point out that their talk can lead to descriptive and poetic writing. Lights back on, everyone returns to work.

Living and teaching requires my presence and attention. Using my own experience in a minilesson gives students a glimpse of who I am. When students

In the artist workshop.

2L: a great artists share.
Respectful. Excellent comments.
Attempts at drawing in contour -
"Miss Ernst, I wrote two   great.
sentences." (Max).

Paul in 2L -
writing.

Claire

Mrs. Cireno
Claire
Jenny
and the flower

working outside today.
Focus on observation and using quiet voices
Caleb did a great drawing. He was really focused.
Glenn decided to make a "combination of trees."
Hallie just told me that she did "buddy AW" with JW.
3rd graders shared how they write to go with pictures. M.S.
hadn't really gotten much writing yet. This
encouraged kids to really write

Wednesday
21

talk and I really listen and, even more important, write it all down, they know that I learn as much as I lead. As I point out the beauty of student talk and suggest ways to write it, draw it, or title it, they have new models to follow. When I take a survey or point out something good, I show that I expect them to be doing meaningful work. Justin asks me what I am going to do with the scrap of paper on which I wrote down what he said. "I'll put it in my journal," I answer, and he nods. Children know what they say and do is important to my teaching.

Connecting Learning and Teaching

Monica Dougherty, a fourth-grade teacher, walks into the artists workshop ahead of her fourth-grade class. "Could I do an artist's share today?" she asks. I recognize her urgency. She places her painting of tiny dots of watercolor on the easel, settles into a chair a distance from the easel, and explains that her idea came from a minilesson about Seurat and pointillism. She became so involved in her picture of a tree in a pumpkin field, against a colorful sky, that she worked on it over the long weekend. "I want to share this," she explains, "because it is the first time I have made a picture from my imagination. I usually copy from a book or an art card."

The class stares at the work of their teacher. Appreciative silence is followed by comments on the beautiful colors of the sunset and the silhouette of the fall tree against the evening sky. Monica raises her hand to clarify. "This isn't a sunset. It is a sunrise. That is very important, because I tried hard to make the pumpkins look like they were shining with morning dew."

"What is the difference between the way sunrise and sunset look?" I ask. A lively conversation follows.

When these fourth graders return to their classroom, Monica follows up on the experience and asks her students to research the difference between sunrise and sunset. In making this assignment, she instantly links science, art, writing, research, and reading. The students' observation journals become important tools.

Monica brings in poetry that describes sunrises and sunsets. She shows her students the section of the newspaper that lists the exact time of sunrise and sunset. They sketch what they see outside their windows, and they write about the subtle differences between the two. Grant's entry, which accompanies a drawing of trees springing from a squiggly ground line, begins, "It is 4:18 and 58 seconds. The sun is setting. The sky is white and the trees look like shadows." Each day members of the class share more observations, more differences, more similarities.

Claire's journal reflects her weeklong focus on the landscape, a week of slowing down to observe the sun setting and rising. "When I looked in the paper to see what time sunset would be, the paper said 4:25. So I went to my window and saw that it was a blackish gray color. I drew my tree and my yard with a black background. In the morning I drew my neighbor's stone gate with an iron gray-blue sky because I saw all of that in my car window." Six days later, as she looks back at her drawings and written observations, she writes two poems:

SUNSET

Pink, purple, blue, red
paint the sky above
the harbor as all the
little boats get tucked
in for bed. As the sun
melts away more colors
bloom, orange, yellow, green,
dark blue. When the sun
finishes melting, dusk is here.

SUNRISE

Blackness, darkness, silence.
Bit by bit, the sun slowly
raises its face, over the horizon.
Its golden rays
shimmer across the water
leading to Compo Beach.
The sounds of birds
break the morning
peace. A dog runs along
the water's edge barking
in the distance. Soon the
first jogger appears.
Day has come.

Through Monica's artist's share, her students see her learning and how it is part of her life, not merely something for school. Her inquiry about sunrise and sunset comes from her interest in science, in the curriculum she is responsible for teaching. That inquiry excites me and shows me other ways that science and art can connect. When teachers come into the art room, they open the door to my learning.

Authentic integration will happen in school when teachers bring with them their expertise in science or math or art or music and go into other classrooms to see things from that view, to establish links, raise questions, extend learning.

Our schools can become laboratories—studios of learning—when we open the doors of our classrooms and learn from one another, take ideas that have

select something in count of 10.
This is our rehearsal. Think about what
you will do. After 5 minutes —
we'll make choices.

Frisk and
"Peter in the
gallery corner"

Tuesday

4

started in art and extend them into science, reading, or math. When we begin to teach how to live—to share a sunrise that we are proud to have captured—we begin to understand that when a child says, "Are we going to do artist's share today?" she means she needs to.

When teachers connect with their own learning and with one another, our students have teams of teachers, schools of teachers, who know them, teach them, and learn with them. Children no longer believe the art teacher belongs only in the art room. Children no longer need to sneak away in order to draw instead of write. Science discoveries, research, and reports can be conveyed through poetry and paintings.

Learning from Mistakes

After everyone makes a choice and goes to work, Steven sits alone on the rug. "I want to do clay today!" he challenges. He knows that this late in the year, clay is not a choice. "I have to use clay to make an owl like the owl in my picture," he explains seriously. His detailed picture of an owl, a blue sky and moon in the background—which he worked on for several weeks—is evidence of his expertise and confidence in art. His focus in the art room is in contrast to his easy distraction in other subjects. His teachers and I wonder what works for him here. I give Steven a ball of clay, but ask him to work on the rug, away from his friends (I don't want to have to defend my decision to give him clay). I worry because I know that going from a two-dimensional work to a three-dimensional one is a great challenge; will he become discouraged? He goes to work, and I never return to the rug.

At cleanup time, Steven approaches me with a tiny flat piece of clay that looks like the letter *v*. "Here," he offers.

"What is it?" I ask.

"A crane. I couldn't do the owl."

As I place it on the clay shelf I wonder what happened, how he will react, whether I made a mistake by giving him clay. I can't tell by looking at the clay, but his writing tells the story.

> *Today I had a rough time. I feel like I wasted my time. I spent thirty minutes trying to figure out how I was going to do a clay work of my owl, fifteen minutes of the rest of the time trying to do it. Nothing came out right. I tried doing it flat and you couldn't even tell it was a bird. I tried it 3-D and it always fell apart. I tried it flying and I tried it on a beach, resting. I don't know why nothing came out right. It might have worked if I had used clay more. It might have worked if I had someone helping me. I ended up with a crane.*

It is flying in the air. The crane took me about two minutes. It is pretty good but it means nothing to me. It is just like going back to first grade. But I didn't talk to anyone. The only thing that will stay in my mind is that I didn't give up. That means something to me. I still haven't given up. I have colored clay at home and I'll try that. It might be a little easier. I know what it should look like now. I won't be rushed. I'll have hours to try. My mom can give ideas and help me to correct things. I think I am still improving. This is another step up to becoming an artist. My mistakes—I can learn from them and not give up.

In workshops where students have projects of their own, where they really care about the outcome, they can learn from their mistakes and learn even bigger lessons in the process. I model my own mistakes in minilessons. Students highlight their mistakes in artist's share. A visiting illustrator once told us that working with your mistakes gives you power.

If teachers show students how to make an owl in clay, how to draw a boat or a tree, will they learn the lesson of not giving up, find determination to keep going, unleash their power? If we look only at the project on the shelf or the picture on the drying rack, will we know what learning occurred? Students teach me that at times they must learn things on their own.

Classrooms must focus on the process of learning, not as the end result but in order to feed into the students' understanding of what they can accomplish. When students write about their process, explain their discoveries, capture a moment of their work in the art room, the focus moves on to other important lessons.

When struggle and challenge are focused on—through sharing, minilessons, conversation, writing, modeling—as intently as the product, students can keep working until they reach their goal.

Constantly Revising

Lynn Gehr and her students are rehearsing for their final artist's share. They decide they will critique one person's work in the hope that it will make everyone's work better. Wally volunteers. He puts several pictures of animals on the easel; a tiger with vibrant orange-and-black lines stands out. "This shows my progress of drawing animals over the year," he says.

"What do you want us to see or understand?" I push. "Don't forget that you have to explain how these pictures and your writing show something. What do they show?"

Wally is on the spot. His classmates sit in silence while Wally thinks. "They show life, color, spirit," he responds. "I made a challenge for myself when I drew animals. The moose was the beginning."

He starts his presentation again, this time talking more clearly, with more purpose. "I want to show my progress over the year. This tiger is alive, waiting to come out."

A classmates ventures, "You seemed a bit shaky."

"I like how you discuss your progress," adds another.

Wally admits, "I need to revise my writing."

Students learn about the need to revise when the talk in a classroom focuses on thinking, when the teacher asks, what do you mean? what is the point? how can you make it clearer? Writing improves when we set deadlines, go public, publish, and have real audiences.

The next day, Wally's animal pictures again grace the easel. He explains how each shows his progress, and he reads his revised piece of writing about the tiger.

> *The tiger looks at me. His eyes are fixed on me like two rocks as he growls. Water trickles in the stream. The misty feeling touches me on the face. I listen to the sound of the rain forest. I hear a frog close by say, "Ribbit," then jump into the stream.*
>
> *A little breeze encounters me for a second. I see a tree frog climbing the tree close to me. I stop for a minute to look at the shadows in the river. I'm about to leave when I see a frog hop into the water. The shadows turn into a blur for a second. Then they go back to the way they were before I came.*
>
> *The sky is a dark blue. I hear a pitter-patter. Then a little monkey emerges from the bush. Then another monkey appears and scoops up the baby and disappears into the trees.*

Writing expands when students hear one another's voices, respond, ask hard questions, tell what they hear, reveal the images they see in their mind as they listen. Pictures are not merely illustrations, they are ideas, a jumping-off point. Revision is hard, and it matters that writing be good.

We need to pay attention to language. We need to stop while we are reading picture books and say, "Wow, listen to those words. Can you see the images in your mind?" When someone talks poetically, point it out. When someone writes a line full of imagery, read it aloud. Reread writing to find lines that others can see. End or begin a workshop by filling the room with lines of student language. Hear language, see language, say language, feel language, in order to help students write with voice, authority, and passion.

Holding Your Journal Still

I speak frankly to a class of third graders, and they wait to see what I will change in the workshop. "I am concerned that you take this connection between making a picture and writing for granted. I worry that when you make a picture it might fill up time and lead to no thought or words." My concern is that we—children and teachers—take things for granted. I know that I must raise questions and break out of the routine to teach my students and myself to pay attention, think, concentrate, and focus on ideas. I constantly revise the workshop by searching for new ways to begin art, teach minilessons on technique, push students to think, maintain quiet.

We begin with five minutes of silent drawing and thinking. "Draw to observe something; concentrate on it," I explain. "Keep your eye on the object, imagine that your pen is touching the duck or owl, and take a journey with your pen. Remember that you are learning to see, not making a beautiful picture."

The room is silent as the third graders draw the preserved animals I have borrowed from the nature center. Leon leans over and turns his head as he tries to capture the seagull. Ben kneels on the floor, occasionally looking at his sketch to see where his pen has been.

After five minutes I call out names one by one and students tell one thing they observed. "It is hard to look down and up." "I have to measure distances." "I can draw better than I thought I could." "If you do all kinds of different scribbles with your pen, you can see a difference." "I could really concentrate." "I noticed how long the tail of the duck is." "I tried not to worry about the texture, just the outline." "If you really stare, you forget everything else." "When I moved my journal, I messed up. I had to hold my journal still."

I feel the excitement in my classroom. Small but important lessons on technique are learned in a short time. This does not take away choice but revises it, confirms the importance of thinking and concentrating in the workshop, learning a new skill. Changing the pace, raising the expectation, are important to keeping a workshop alive.

We need to hold our journals still as we pay attention, question, and worry. We need to know that the tension we feel, that sense of being off balance, will lead to learning. We need to share our frustrations with our students. We need to ask hard questions and find answers to those questions. We need to talk to our colleagues, turn our worries into new ideas for our classroom. We need to acknowledge the importance of concentration. We need to change the routine, make exceptions, notice when someone needs to share, and stay open to surprise. We need to model our own learning in life to bring life to our classroom.

Nicholas brings in a
skull. I'm going to
draw it. He went
upstairs to get
his picture. "I want to
revise it." 3A has been
working on revision
on their pictures

Marc: why picked clay
"Clay" — For the second
time in my life.
I wanted to see if
I was better than in
1st grade.

Marc —
Should I have forced you to
do clay? Yes — I could've
gotten better at it. That way I
wouldn't have worked in my
sketch journal each time.

We need to put ourselves and our students on the spot, rethink, revise, and establish higher expectations. We need to pay attention.

Experience for Yourself

- Draw an object that you observe. Keep your pen on the paper and your eye on the object. Draw in silence for five minutes. Afterward, write down everything you noticed.
- Make a list of the lessons you learned from the stories in this chapter.
- Write about a time when you learned something. What was the important lesson? Translate the learning in that experience into a lesson for your classroom.

13

Changing History

As I look into my picture I can see the drawing I did in second grade. It is like going back in time. I can see Mrs. Gehr and me side by side, staring at Raggedy Ann and drawing her. It is a memory in my drawing.

—Courtney, age 10

Children represent their stories with pictures. When they enter school at age four or five, crayons and paints are their tools for literacy, self-expression, meaning. We read them the words of a picture book as they read the pictures; the pictures remind them of the words as we reread it.

When classroom teachers see the pictures of children, listen to their thinking and meaning and the clarity of their voices in the context of art, they begin to understand the connection between art and learning. By making their own pictures, teachers can fill years of blank white pages, forget their fear that someone will say, "That's not right," dismiss the idea that they can't carry a sketch journal because they aren't an artist. Teachers quickly learn that they can begin by copying something, that time seems endless while they are concentrating on a picture, that making a picture can stir up emotions and memories, that there is a lot to write about after they finish.

When teachers, in collaboration, believe a picture is a means of expression and put that belief into practice, we will change our own learning history and that of our students. We will no longer ask students to stop making pictures and move on to words. We will know that they can continue to use pictures as reminders, see a story in a painting, draw their observations and questions, and connect verbal images with visual ones. When students use sketch journals to draw what they see, what they notice will change the way they think and write. School will look different from when we grew up.

This change doesn't happen overnight, after reading one book, nor can it be brought about by following someone else's plan. It happens over time, begins with one person, and expands as teachers and parents inquire into the knowledge and meaning of children. When schoolchildren continue to practice what they know when they enter school, the culture of the school changes.

When visitors enter our school, they immediately notice the calm, the consistency of belief, and the collaboration that takes place among the teachers and the children. Visit our school and see what I mean. Think about how it differs from the school you attended or the one in which you now teach. Think about how you can begin to change history in your classroom.

Seeing in New Ways

My students change the way I see teaching and learning, and that changes my history as a teacher and learner. Matthew sits in the chair ready to talk about the picture he has chosen for the final artist's share of his second-grade year. His classmates and I focus on an orange, black-splotched painting on the easel. Silence falls as I think about Matthew's history as a learner—shy, difficulty in reading, writing, math. I rarely see the meaning in his pictures, even though he seems to enjoy making them. I think this opportunity to share must be a challenge for him.

Matthew describes his picture: "This is the best picture I have made this year. It is a cheetah about to catch a koala bear for his dinner."

Without thinking, I interrupt. "Matthew, what are you talking about? I don't see a cheetah or a koala bear!" I see only the orange, the black splotches, and a figure or shape in a circle in the middle of the page.

"It is the eye of the cheetah, and the koala bear is right in the middle of his eye. He is about ready to pounce on it," Matthew responds with boldness and clarity.

I am the last to understand Matthew's picture. All of his classmates immediately see the huge eye filling the page and the reflection of the tiny koala in the middle. These seven- and eight-year-olds have not lost the abilty to read a picture, see meaning in it. They think about what they draw and paint, write about it. This gives them a foundation from which to approach other students' pictures or works of professional artists and find their own meaning.

Even though writing and drawing in my sketch journal is the way I see, learn, reflect, and take in the world of my classroom, my history as an artist, writer, learner, thinker did not include those tools from the begining. My history did not include learning to see, to value art and pictures in my literacy, did not include the idea that art is as important as reading and writing and math, that there is meaning beyond the surface of a picture. Children know instinctively that a picture is a story, that a picture can help them find their voice, and that pictures in combination with writing can help them imagine, create, think, see, wonder, understand, and communicate.

Matthew's picture is now part of his learning history. It is a product of his imagination. His words make it come alive, his story is important, and artist's share gives him the deadline and the place to say it, show it.

When art is part of literacy, students have new ways to see, multiple ways to say things; the combination means that students like Matthew, who have difficulty reading and writing, can find a way to be part of the learning community.

Admiting Success

Wally, preparing for his artist's share, sits in the chair staring at his own picture on the easel. He spontaneously exclaims, "Wow! I didn't know I could make such a good picture!"

Cliff tells a visitor, "I'm known for my flowers." Justine, Giancarlo, and Emily are known for their animals. Kindergartners sprawl on the floor copying the works of older students. Students copy down the words of artists to inspire them.

The pictures on the bulletin board in the sharing area tell stories about the people who created them—Sam filled in the whole page, Natasha tried something new, Andrew turned a mistake into a success, Anna is an expert at shading. The pictures on display do not imply that there is a best or a worst but that each person can strive and teach a lesson to everyone else.

Children make art part of their learning and culture, know they can say "wow" when they look at their own work, smile wide when they ask, "Do you like it?" and really mean "I love it." In artists workshop students learn that they can all be artists in some way and instead of losing confidence, instead of telling the story of when they learned they couldn't, they find ways to use their success and confidence in other areas of learning—writing a poem, using a sketch journal in science, using a picture to revise their writing. We support, announce, and celebrate success to create a community in which we can accept criticism and improve.

Critiquing Kindly

Deborah responds to one of her classmates during another artist's share. "Bring the grass up and the sky down," she suggests. When two children sprawl on the rug, one copying a dragon by an eighth grader, the other copying van Gogh's *Starry Night,* they move up to the originals and talk about where a line goes, how he needs to make the eyes differently, how she can make the sky look like it is swirling with stars.

Tyler.
drawing
under the
dragon's eye.

Learning to look at our own and others' work with a critical eye in a community that supports risk taking, we are able to give and take criticism, raise expectations, and design appropriate outcomes. Artist's share, author's chair—sharing as an integral part of the classroom—gives students a forum, teaches them to talk about and listen to what they see and think. By listening to children—making them our informants—instead of teaching them what we know, we see our own world and what is important in their learning differently.

Sharing is important, and in the beginning, responses should be positive— tell others what you notice, what works, what ideas you gain. That way children build confidence, improve. Sky depicted as a thin blue line across the top of a page becomes a blue-and-white space with a horizon because teachers and students are saying, *Tell me about it, tell me what it is. What do you mean? Step back so you can see your own picture from a distance.* There is no right or wrong, but there is a clear expectation that there is room for improvement.

Making It Your Own

Toward the end of fourth grade, Brian writes, "This year I am very good at poetry and chalk pastel . . . [but] I find that I haven't expanded my life in art. I have only discovered fifty percent of my abilities. I only know half of what I am wanting to know."

Rosie returns to the artists workshop after a five-week absence and chooses to continue working on a picture she began many weeks before.

Samantha writes, "When other people are satisfied and you aren't, you should keep going until you are. Some things you learn from reading books or listening to teachers, but the good things are the things you find out by yourself, by trying new things."

Students sustain interest in projects over time, work with purpose, take small steps and make huge strides in learning, because their work matters to them. These students know that their ideas are at the center of the workshop and learn to be self-critical instead of only asking the teacher, "Do you like it?" They are not left alone to do as they choose but are asked to make choices in a context in which choice has been taught. Whenever I see a first or second grader holding a picture up for a friend's perusal, I know they understand that they must critique themselves in order to keep going—I hope for a lifetime.

Including Others

When apprenticeship, sharing, and response are part of the workshop or classroom, the learning history of a child includes the works of others. For his final artist's share in fourth grade, John chooses his drawing of a car to show how his work has changed and progressed. "I saw a picture like this when I was in first grade. It popped into my head again now, so I made it."

"That was by Brian!" I interrupt with excitement. Brian is in John's fourth-grade class and is part of John's inspiration. When Dawn Damiani learns that a fourth grader has copied a picture of hers displayed on the bulletin board, she admits that it is the first time in her life anyone ever copied her work. Nicole, a fourth grader, writes, "I got my idea from second grade and a picture my teacher made in her sketch journal." When third grader Vikas wants to help his kindergarten buddy get an idea for their joint writers workshop, he leads him by the hand to the artists workshop and shows him his leopard picture.

Students are teachers who have access to a wealth of knowledge and ideas. The history of children and teachers includes the pictures and ideas they acquire from one another. Cary's lion, a white tiger by Justine, a fall moon, the eye of a cheetah, are pictures that anchor and challenge so many students as they work. The combined pictures of all the children and teachers hold the history of the artists workshop and the school.

Seeing for Yourself

When teachers make pictures of their own, it changes the way they see and the way they teach. Monica Dougherty, a fourth-grade teacher, shares a picture of a tiger from her sketch journal in her final artist's share of the year:

> *This process helps me as a teacher. If I stay with one picture for a long time, it helps me understand artists more. When I draw, I think more, understand things, like drawing something in a reflection makes it distorted. I have taught in other schools where kids would write, then illustrate their stories. But when I started to make my own pictures this year, I began to see the world differently. I began to notice how furniture is arranged, how the light hits the plants in my doctor's office. It has made me a much more careful observer. It has come entirely from making my own pictures.*

A student responds spontaneously, "I know how you feel."

Lynn Gehr explains how joining her second-grade class in making pictures changed her thinking. "First of all, I became an artist. I never considered myself one—just crafty, not good at drawing. I considered myself good at bulletin boards but I would never go any further."

When teachers do an artist's share, they inform and connect with children. When teachers meet in study groups or communities of learning, they begin to take risks, ask questions, find their public voice, collaborate with parents, change things—their classrooms, their own learning history, the learning history of the children they teach.

Teaching Parents

Parents learn along with children and teachers. When I tell a class that "adults are scared to make pictures," the students say they know why: "They are afraid of making a mistake." "They don't have any ideas." "Someone might have told them they weren't good." A parent who is volunteering in the art room stops washing paint palettes and listens. When I do a minilesson on drawing to see, a parent moves over and sits at the edge of the rug to learn along with the class.

Parents have an investment in school. They want to help, and they want to understand why school is not the way it was when they were children. We need to invite them to particpate, make them part of the partnership. They know the fear of blank white pages, they remember being told what to see, not how. They remember *separate, best, worst, can* or *can't*. When they listen to children talk about art, they begin to see what art means, get the nerve to try a picture for themselves, see things differently. Children, teachers, and parents must learn together, and in doing so they can revise education together.

Expecting More

There is no best; it is always changing because we build on what we learn together. There are always higher expectations and tougher questions to help us change. Individual pictures become exemplars to move beyond. Individual pieces are part of a bigger whole. We must look at portfolios and sketch journals, writing in process, published writing. All these things show the person and their range of thinking.

Let's look at two pages in Ben's journal. One has a sketch of his favorite stuffed animal and some revealing commentary: "It gives me a sense of security. The neck can't support the head anymore because I hugged him by the neck. Now he is someone to talk to that can't think. Sometimes I have him ride on my shoulders." The other page is filled with questions: "What is the scientific name for our sun? Does our planet have a scientific name other than Earth? What are the odds of there being a tenth planet?"

Range does not increase and best does not change and broaden when students are left on their own. When teachers direct their lessons, give leads for writing, ask questions for which they don't have answers, give assignments, establish structures, find ways to use sketch journals across the curriculum, draw in science class, and write in art class, they open the door to the whole learner. They open the way to the imagination, to scientific thought, to observation, to emotion.

Expanding Writing

When art is part of the writers workshop, teachers must create structures so that children know that improved writing is the focus. Walking around a classroom, looking at open sketch journals, I notice an intricate drawing of a wicker chair, which fills an entire page of Brian's journal. I comment, "Great drawing, Brian," and move on. He follows me, whispering: "You're supposed to read the writing, Ms. Ernst."

When Peter von Euler asks his fourth graders to write a series of memories of their years at our school, many students focus their memories by drawing a picture. Brian draws a picture of the stairs going to the second floor, because it was there he told his best friend he was moving. Alex draws a picture of the small bush he sees each morning as he gets off the bus. Mark draws the telephone in the office because in first grade that was the way he could contact his mom. Dan draws the door to the nurse's office, a place where he felt safe when he was in first grade. The pictures help students make contact with a memory and bring a presence to the writing.

Darcy Hicks and her students find that reseeing a picture helps them learn the art of revising their writing. Changing the picture helps them change the story. Amelia lifts the layers of her work pinned on the board in her classroom. She explains that her original idea came from a picture she made in second grade. She shows one page and then another filled with the marks she made on her own writing to change it. Colin says, "I revised twice. Revising the picture gives me ideas for my writing." He points to a picture, an "experiment," that led him to a piece of writing that gave him the idea that the picture could be a forest fire. Connections such as these revise teaching.

Connecting Learning and Teaching

Children need to go public, get feedback, teach, learn, and make their own connections. Teachers' doors must be always open, they must be willing to revise their plan on a moment's notice. Alisa comes to the art room to continue a picture and piece of writing she started in her third-grade writers workshop. When I am teaching a third-grade class, first graders from Mary Sue Welch's room walk into the art room to read the stories they wrote in writers workshop. We read their writing instead of the story I had planned. The older students respond and then applaud.

When Jonathan sees me in the hallway in the morning, he drops his backpack and pulls out his sketch journal to show me what he drew the night before. Samantha walks into the art room and asks, "Can I read you what I wrote in my sketch journal? I think you will like it."

Amelia —

"Today I'm going to draw mountains with snow on
top: a field of daffodils. The wind howling hard.
I'll make red colors in the sky —

Why everyone uses calm blue skies — it's diff. Now I
do wild skies. I go to the beach. The sky was blue
and the clouds were bright pink —

Roared — the clouds and sun having a fight.
My name is Daisy. I am a mountain.
You have to stop shining all that light on me.
    the cloud whined.
I can't help it, the sun bellowed.

Maybe the fireflies can help. She points to the
grass for us to see the tiny flies in gold crayon.

I used my sketch journal
to get ideas for my picture.
and for writing:

Amelia lifts
the layers of
her work.

Colin stood by and brought
Amelia her next piece

"Now it looks like the
wind blowing."
I got the idea from a
book but I changed it
a little.

she describes
in detail how her
picture is
diff.
from the
book.

Visiting teachers ask how they can make this happen in their schools. I answer, *Create assignments, establish specific structures in the classroom, and work with your colleagues who hold similar beliefs. It will allow all of you to keep learning and be teachers of all of the students in your school.*

Broadening art across the curriculum does not diminish my role as the art specialist but increases its importance. Art leads to closer observation, encourages critical thinking, and triggers more expressive and descriptive writing. What students experience in their classroom writers workshop differs from what they experience in the artists workshop, but the two venues are clearly linked.

"This isn't about adding, it is about taking a step back, looking at the role of art through another lens, going back to a more natural state," suggests a visitor. Making art more central to learning is not adding a new structure to your classroom, it is restructuring how you see, think, learn, and teach. It is integration, in the authentic and natural way that children understand in the beginning of their history as learners. I hope these stories have changed the way you think about what is possible and will help you sketch your own plan to change the history of the students you teach.

Experience for Yourself

- Make a picture that tells a story. Write the story. Show the picture to a colleague and ask them to tell the story that they are reminded of as they look at your picture.
- Relook at your picture. What could you add or change? Revise the picture and revise the writing.
- Make a sketch of your own classroom. Revise the sketch. Think of what new things are possible or what needs to change.

14

Sketching Your Own Plan

I think that one of the biggest things I'll remember from this year was the first day I got my observation journal. I thought the whole idea was pointless, and I couldn't understand what the teachers were trying to get at. The next day, the whole thing came to me. They wanted us to get inspirations for writing from pictures that we made. From then on, I started drawing and writing and drawing and writing, and so on. From that point it was like I was a whole new person. And that's something I'll never forget.

—Alex, age 10

Keep a sketch journal. Take it with you everywhere. Fill the pages with drawings of and writing about what you see, hear, think, and feel. Draw and write every day—capture the moments of your life and of your classroom.

Use you sketch journal to practice looking and drawing. Forget about someone looking over your shoulder and begin to figure out your own process—what works, what doesn't, what feels exciting.

Share your learning with your students. They need to see you as a learner, someone who uses the things you teach. Pay close attention to your students, listen to them talk, ask them questions, and write it all down in your journal. Let the answers they give you be the information that propels your teaching.

Share your learning with a colleague or two. Form a community of teachers to learn, wonder, read, write, and share together. You will begin to feel the support of that community. Turn to them with your questions, appropriate their ideas. Then take their ideas and the ideas in this book, filter them through your learning and your passion, and invent your own way, sketch your own plan. Your classroom will bear the imprint of your collaboration, it will become a community.

Collect quotes from writers and artists and combine them with the knowledge of scientists and historians. Don't let the boundaries that existed in your own learning get in your way. Ask the art or music teacher for their expertise. Ask them in, invite them to learn with you.

Let art books and reproductions inspire and inform the work that goes on in your journal and your classroom. Let your students know that you have mentors and colleagues, that without them the learning community in your classroom is incomplete. Urge your students to be mentors to one another.

Redesign your own workshop based on what you are learning. Establish routines so that students know what to expect; encourage them to create and imagine within the structures you define. Expect them to go beyond your boundaries, and begin to widen the frame of learning and literacy.

Place choice at the center of what you do. Just as you may need to start by copying from a picture book, imitating the voice of an author, or using another person's idea, students may need to start there too. Always demonstrate technique, model other ways, and show where to find answers. Be open to the possibility that there is another way than the one you thought of. Be clear that choice is not freedom but holds great responsibility—theirs and yours. Prepare for the challenges it brings.

Give students their own sketch journals. Find ways to guide their use: to record a vacation, to gather ideas, to look at the details, to respond to literature, to develop and invent ideas. Remind them that artists, writers, and scientists need a journal, need to draw and write in order to think about and develop their craft.

Take your students with their journals to an art museum to help them understand how they can learn about their history, culture, and themselves by reading a painting. Give them reason to go to museums for a lifetime, make sure they know that they can stand before a work of art and learn—discover technique, uncover an emotion, find a story—and that their sketches and jottings can lead to a poem, a painting, or scientific wondering.

Remind them that keeping a sketch journal is not confined to "artists" but can extend anyone's ability to observe and think. It is not a hobby but a way of taking in, imagining, opening the mind, solving a problem, leaping to a new idea, returning to a memory. It is not disconnected from but connected to life and learning. It can be carried proudly and opened for others to see.

Tell them stories connected to their life of learning. Tell them that when I was on vacation I sat in a restaurant drawing a birch tree outside the window. A woman watched me and said, "I'm an artist. I wish I had the nerve to draw in a sketch journal in public." Tell them about my friend, an editor, who said that she worried that if someone saw her drawing they might tap her on the shoulder and say, "Excuse me, you are not an artist." Tell them I know a group of teachers who took their sketch journals to a beach and were surrounded by children. When one child said, "You are artists, aren't you?," the teachers did not know how to answer.

Tell these stories to help your students know they can continue to say *Yes, I am* or *Yes, I can*. Artists, editors, and teachers can draw in public, thereby showing that it is necessary and important to their life and work. This does not take away from the people who choose to be artists, but expands the ability of the work of artists to inform us all—to change our life.

Turn the hallways of your school into galleries, make them new spaces for teaching and learning, not places for decoration. Require that everyone select a piece, and explain the process whereby the work got there. Step back and watch the exhibit propel work to new heights.

Make time for sharing. When a student asks, "Will there be artist's [or writer's or scientist's] share, recognize that question as a need to go public. Let your students hear your voice as you tell about a picture, explain what you learned from a mistake you made, talk about a book you read, or point out what you discover in a piece of writing. Let your voice come through in your writing and teaching. Find your public voice.

Educate everyone in your community. Invite parents into your classroom, explain what you are doing, give them something to do, ask them to make their own picture and write about it. Let experience become their teacher, and watch them become your advocate for change.

Always assess. Assess as you move through the room writing down what your students say. Assess as you listen to a student in an artist's share, as portfolios go home, as you ask questions because you really need the answers, as you look at an exhibition, as you revise your teaching.

Make the frame of learning larger, open to more possibilities. If you are a classroom teacher, visit the art teacher. If you are an art or a music teacher, visit a classroom workshop. Use your expertise as a lens through which to look at an art, science, math, music, or writing lesson in order to connect it to what you do. Together with others—teachers, students, and parents—change history. Change what it means to integrate the curriculum and make art central to learning.

Use your sketch journal as your new text for learning and teaching. Experience it yourself. Sketch your own plan.

Susan sharing his story
in Author's Sharing in.
Mrs Cereno's class

Bibliography

Professional Literature

Atwell, N. 1987. *In the Middle: Writing, Reading, and Learning with Adolescents*. Portsmouth, NH: Boynton/Cook.

Barbieri, M., and C. Tateishi, eds. 1996. *Meeting the Challenges: Stories from Today's Classroom*. Portsmouth, NH: Heinemann.

Benedict, S., and L. Carlisle, eds. 1992. *Beyond Words:Picture Books for Older Readers and Writers*. Portsmouth, NH: Heinemann.

Berthoff, A. E. 1984. *Reclaiming the Imagination*. Portsmouth, NH: Boynton/Cook.

Boyer, E. 1995. *The Basic School: A Community for Learning*. Princeton, NJ: The Carnegie Foundation.

Bridges, L. 1996. *Creating Your Classroom Community*. York, ME: Stenhouse.

Calkins, L. 1994. *The Art of Teaching Writing*. Portsmouth, NH: Heinemann.

Calkins, L., and S. Harwayne. 1990. *Living Between the Lines*. Portsmouth, NH: Heinemann.

Chancer, J., and G. Rester-Zodrow. 1997. *Moon Journals: Writing, Art, and Inquiry Through Focused Nature Study*. Portsmouth, NH: Heinemann.

Cohen, E.P, and R. S. Gainer. 1995. *Art: Another Language for Learning*. Portsmouth, NH: Heinemann.

Coles, R. 1992. *Their Eyes Meeting the World: The Drawings and Paintings of Children*. Boston: Houghton Mifflin.

Drummond, M. 1994. *Learning to See: Assessment Through Observation*. York, ME: Stenhouse.

Eisner, E. 1992. "The Misunderstood Role of the Arts in Human Development." *Phi Delta Kappan* (April): 591–95.

Ernst, K. 1994. *Picturing Learning: Artists and Writers in the Classroom*. Portsmouth, NH: Heinemann.

Fisher, B. 1995. *Thinking and Learning Together*. Portsmouth, NH: Heinemann.

Fletcher, R. 1996. *Breathing In, Breathing Out: Keeping a Writer's Notebook*. Portsmouth, NH: Heinemann.

———. 1993. *What a Writer Needs*. Portsmouth, NH: Heinemann.

Fraser, J., and D. Skolnick. 1994. *On Their Way: Celebrating Second Graders as They Read and Write*. Portsmouth, NH: Heinemann.

Gallas, K. 1994. *The Languages of Learning: How Children Talk, Write, Dance, Draw, and Sing Their Understanding of the World*. New York: Teachers College Press.

Gardner, H. 1991. *The Unschooled Mind: How Children Think and How Schools Should Teach*. New York: Basic Books.

Graves, D. 1994. *A Fresh Look at Writing*. Portsmouth, NH: Heinemann.

———. 1983. *Writing: Teachers and Children at Work*. Portsmouth, NH: Heinemann.

Greene, M. 1995. *Releasing the Imagination: Essays on Education, the Arts, and Social Change*. New York: Teachers College Press.

———. 1988. *The Dialectic of Freedom*. New York: Teachers College Press.

———. 1978. *Landscapes of Learning*. New York: Teachers College Press.

Harste, J., V. Woodward, and C. Burke. 1994. *Language Stories and Literacy Lessons*. Portsmouth, NH: Heinemann.

Harwayne, S. 1992. *Lasting Impressions: Weaving Literature into the Writing Workshop*. Portsmouth, NH: Heinemann.

Heard, G. 1995. *Writing Toward Home: Tales and Lessons to Find Your Way*. Portsmouth, NH: Heinemann.

———. 1989. *For the Good of the Earth and Sun: Teaching Poetry*. Portsmouth, NH: Heinemann.

Hindley, J. 1996. *In the Company of Children*. York, ME: Stenhouse.

Hjerter, K., ed. 1986. *Doubly Gifted: The Author as Visual Artist*. New York: Harry N. Abrams.

Hubbard, R. 1996. *A Workshop of the Possible: Nurturing Children's Creative Development*. York, ME: Stenhouse.

———. 1989. *Authors of Pictures, Draughtsmen of Words*. Portsmouth, NH: Heinemann.

Hubbard, R., and K. Ernst, eds. 1996. *New Entries: Learning by Writing and Drawing*. Portsmouth, NH: Heinemann.

Hubbard, R., and B. Power. 1993. *The Art of Classroom Inquiry: A Handbook for Teacher-Researchers*. Portsmouth, NH: Heinemann.

John-Steiner, V. 1985. *Notebooks of the Mind: Explorations of Thinking*. Albuquerque: University of New Mexico Press.

Johnson, P. 1997. *Pictures and Words Together: Children Illustrating and Writing Their Own Books*. Portsmouth, NH: Heinemann.

London, P. 1994. *Step Outside: Community-Based Art Education*. Portsmouth, NH: Heinemann.

McPhail, David. 1996. *In Flight with David McPhail: A Creative Autobiography*. Portsmouth, NH: Heinemann.

Miletta, M. 1996. *A Multiage Classroom: Choice and Possibility*. Portsmouth, NH: Heinemann.

Moline, S. 1995. *I See What You Mean*. York, ME: Stenhouse.

Murray, D. 1996. *Crafting a Life: In Essay, Story, Poem*. Portsmouth, NH: Boynton/Cook.

———. 1989. *Expecting the Unexpected: Teaching Myself—and Others—to Read and Write*. Portsmouth, NH: Boynton/Cook.

Newkirk, T., ed. 1994. *Workshop 5: The Writing Process Revisited*. Portsmouth, NH: Heinemann.

———, ed. 1992. *Workshop 4: The Teacher as Researcher*. Portsmouth, NH: Heinemann.

Olson, J. 1992. *Envisioning Writing: Toward an Integration of Drawing and Writing*. Portsmouth, NH: Heinemann.

Power, B. 1996. *Taking Note: Improving Your Observational Notetaking*. York, ME: Stenhouse.

Rief, L. 1992. *Seeking Diversity: Language Arts with Adolescents*. Portsmouth, NH: Heinemann.

Robinson, G. 1996. *Sketch-Books: Explore and Store*. Portsmouth, NH: Heinemann.

Romano, T. 1995. *Writing with Passion: Life Stories, Multiple Genres*. Portsmouth, NH: Heinmann.

Routman, R. 1996. *Literacy at the Crossroads: Crucial Talk About Reading, Writing, and Other Teaching Dilemmas*. Portsmouth, NH: Heinemann.

———. 1994. *Invitations: Changing as Teachers and Learners K-12, with updated, expanded, and revised Resources and Blue Pages*. Portsmouth, NH: Heinemann.

Short, K., J. Harste, and C. Burke. 1995. *Creating Classrooms for Authors and Inquirers*. Portsmouth, NH: Heinemann.

Whitin, P. 1997. *Inquiry at the Window: Pursuing the Wonders of Learners*. Portsmouth, NH: Heinemann.

———. 1996. *Sketching Stories, Stretching Minds*. Portsmouth, NH: Heinemann.

Children's Literature

Anholt, L. 1996. *Degas and the Little Dancer*. Toronto, London: Barrons.

———. 1994. *Camille and the Sunflowers*. Hauppaug, NY: Barrons.

Baylor, B. 1986. *I Am in Charge of Celebrations*. Illustrated by Peter Parnall. New York: Charles Scribner's Sons.

———. 1977. *The Way to Start a Day*. Illustrated by Peter Parnall. New York: Charles Scribner's Sons.

Berger, B. 1990. *Gwinna*. New York: Philomel.

Bunting, E. 1993. *Red Fox Running*. Paintings by Wendell Minor. New York: Clarion.

Burton, Albert. 1996. *Journey of the Nightly Jaguar*. Illustrated by Robert Roth. New York: Atheneum.

Carle, E. 1991. *Dragons, Dragons and Other Creatures that Never Were*. Compiled by Laura Whipple. New York: Scholastic.

———. 1989. *Animals, Animals*. New York: Philomel Books.

Collins, P. 1992. *I Am an Artist*. Illustrated by Robin Brickman. Brookfield, CT: The Millbrook Press.

Craighead George, J. 1995. *To Climb a Waterfall*. Illustrated by Thomas Locker. New York: Philomel Books.

Dahl, R. 1988. *Matilda*. New York: Viking Kestrel.

———. 1961. *James and the Giant Peach*. New York: Knopf.

De Paola, T. 1989. *The Art Lesson*. New York: G. P. Putnam's Sons.

Doherty, B. 1995. *The Magic Bicycle*. Illustrated by Christian Birmingham. New York: Crown.

Finzel, J. 1991. *Large as Life*. New York: Lothrop, Lee & Shepard Books.

Fleming, D. 1993. *In the Small, Small Pond*. New York: Henry Holt and Company.

Fox, M. 1996. *Zoo Looking*. Illustrated by Candace Whitman. New York: Scholastic.

Frank, J. 1990. *Snow Toward Evening*. Paintings by Thomas Locker. New York: Dial.

Glass, A. 1982. *Jackson Makes His Move*. New York: Frederick Warne.

Gramatky, H. 1989. *Little Toot and the Loch Ness Monster*. New York: G. P. Putnam's Sons.

———. 1939. *Little Toot*. New York: G. P. Putnam's Sons.

Hall, D. 1994. *I Am the Dog. I Am the Cat*. Illustrated by B. Moser. New York: Dial Books.

Hines, A. G. 1994. *What Joe Saw*. New York: Greenwillow Books.

Kesselman, W. 1980. *Emma*. Illustrated by Barbara Cooney. New York: Dell.

Kidd, R. 1996. *Almost Famous Daisy*. New York: Simon and Schuster.

Killion, B. 1982. *The Same Wind*. Illustrated by B. B. Falk. New York: Harper's Children's Books.

Lerner, C. 1994. *Backyard Birds of Winter*. New York: Morrow.

Lionni, L. 1967. *Frederick*. New York: Alfred A. Knopf.

Martin, R., and E. Young. 1985. *Foolish Rabbit's Big Mistake*. New York: G. P. Putnam's Sons.

Moss, S. 1995. *Peter's Painting*. Illustrated by Meredith Thomas. New York: Mondo.

Pinkwater, D. 1977. *The Big Orange Splot*. New York: Scholastic.

Polacco, P. 1991. *Appelemando's Dream*. New York: Philomel Books.

Reiser, L. 1996. *Beach Feet*. New York: Greenwillow Books.

Ringgold, F. 1991. *Tar Beach*. New York: Crown.

Ryder, J. 1993. *The Goodbye Walk*. Illustrated by Deborah Haeffele. New York: Lodestar.

———. 1960. *Earthdance*. Illustrated by Norman Gorbaty. New York: Henry Holt.

Rylant, C. 1995. *The Van Gogh Cafe*. San Diego: Harcourt Brace and Company.

———. 1988. *All I See*. Illustrated by Peter Catalanotto. New York: Orchard Books.

Siebert, D. 1989. *Heartland*. Paintings by Wendell Minor. New York: Thomas Y. Crowell.

Singer, M. 1992. *Chester the Out-of-Work Dog*. Illustrated by Cat Bowman-Smith. New York: Henry Holt.

Stanley, D. 1996. *Leonardo Da Vinci*. New York: Morrow Junior Books.

Tord, B. 1995. *A Blue Butterfly*. New York: Doubleday.

Wallwork, A. 1993. *No Dodos: A Counting Book of Endangered Animals*. New York: Scholastic.

Walsh, E. S. 1989. *Mouse Paint*. San Diego: Harcourt Brace Jovanovich.

Young, E. 1992. *Seven Blind Mice*. New York: Philomel Books.

Drawing is a life-line for me. I
wanted to capture Pepper's black-eyed
staring   head turned down ready
for a scratch! It has rained
hard today and now at 5:00 I
built a fire. Pepper huddled on
the hearth next to Augie —
Isaura sits in the tiny rocker —
perfect for fire watching.

May Sat
3